The Black I

AFRICAN AMERICAN LITERATURE AND CULTURE

EXPANDING AND EXPLODING THE BOUNDARIES

Carlyle V. Thompson
General Editor

Vol. 2

PETER LANG
New York • Washington, D.C./Baltimore • Bern
Frankfurt am Main • Berlin • Brussels • Vienna • Oxford

Devon Boan

The Black "I"

Author and Audience
in African American Literature

PETER LANG
New York • Washington, D.C./Baltimore • Bern
Frankfurt am Main • Berlin • Brussels • Vienna • Oxford

Library of Congress Cataloging-in-Publication Data

Boan, Devon.
The Black "I": author and audience in African American literature / Devon Boan.
p. cm. — (African American literature and culture;. vol. 2)
Includes bibliographical references and index.
1. American literature—African American authors—History and criticism—Theory, etc.
2. Authors and readers—United States—History. 3. African Americans in literature.
4. Reader-response criticism. 5. Self in literature. I. Title. II. Series.
PS153.N5 B565   810.9'896073—dc21   2001038489
ISBN 0-8204-5737-X
ISSN 1528-3887

Die Deutsche Bibliothek-CIP-Einheitsaufnahme

Boan, Devon:
The Black "I": author and audience in African American literature / Devon Boan.
—New York; Washington, D.C./Baltimore; Bern;
Frankfurt am Main; Berlin; Brussels; Vienna; Oxford: Lang.
(African American literature and culture; Vol. 2)
ISBN 0-8204-5737-X

Cover design by Joni Holst

The paper in this book meets the guidelines for permanence and durability
of the Committee on Production Guidelines for Book Longevity
of the Council of Library Resources.

© 2002 Peter Lang Publishing, Inc., New York

Printed in the United States of America

To Kay, John, Jordan, and Madison

With love and gratitude

Table of Contents

Acknowledgments

An author incurs many intellectual debts in the writing of a book, and this book is no exception. At various stages in the book's development, I was privileged by having mentors, teachers, colleagues, and friends offer comments and critical evaluations of its chapters. The book is significantly stronger because of the help of four people in particular—Meili Steele, Judith James, Dianne Johnson, and Amittai Aviram. Several of the chapters were originally drafted as assignments in their classes, and as the book began to shape several years later, their advice and suggestions played an invaluable role in the clarity and cohesion of the theory I am proposing. They are four good people, and four good mentors; I will not forget their encouragement and patient guidance throughout the writing process. They have always had my deep respect, and I am honored by their friendship.

The demands of a project this intense would not have been possible without the support of my wife, Kay, and children, John, Jordan, and Madison. Our family trips, the days together at tennis tournaments or baseball games, the birthday parties, or the quiet evenings alone with Kay were always more satisfying than a night at the computer or in the library, and had the unique ability to make the writing of this book seem like a distraction from the real life I have when I am with them. I think they know of my love for them, but I write it out here so that others will know.

Belmont University, where I have taught for almost six years now, has been a wonderful and supportive place for a scholar to work. The intellectual stimulation and encouraging friendship of its faculty, honors students, staff, and leadership have made the writing of this book easier, and the faculty and staff of the Honors Program—Joseph Byrne, Jonathan Thorndike, and Toma Kimbro—have done an extraordinary job of moving the program to the next level during the time this book was being written. Being a part of such a team is a pleasure; leading them is an honor.

Finally, Chapter 4 has appeared in a somewhat different form in *African American Review* 32.2 (1998): 263–71. I appreciate the guidance the editors gave in the completion of that manuscript, and their willingness to allow its inclusion in this work.

Introduction

The African American Writer's Dilemma

…as minority group children learn the inferior status to which they are assigned—as they observe the fact that they are almost always segregated and kept apart from others who are treated with more respect by the society as a whole—they often react with feelings of inferiority and a sense of personal humiliation. Many of them become confused about their own personal worth….Not every child, of course, reacts with the same patterns of behavior.
—Thurgood Marshall, Supreme Court Brief,
Brown v. Board of Education

For over a century before Thurgood Marshall argued the effects of racial segregation before the Supreme Court, African American authors understood the challenge of writing under the stigma of a racial identity. They were not simply "authors"; they knew that whatever they wrote, in spite of the "racelessness" of the written word, would be measured by expectations white Americans had of both "Negroes" and literature. Conversely, they knew that their self-identities, their stories, and a second audience for whom they wrote were all part of a different America, black America, with its own expectations of itself and its role in white America. The result is that African American writers have exercised their artistic talents with full knowledge that the result would be read one way by white audiences (often well-meaning patrons, but always including critics and even racists) and perhaps an entirely different way by black audiences (with much the same composition). Not surprisingly then, black authors through the last century and a half have woven their literary tapestries with results much like the quilt in Alice Walker's "Everyday Use," a combination of art and instrumentality perverted by the unavoidably political issues of race, economics, and tradition.

W.E.B. Du Bois, in his 1903 classic *The Souls of Black Folk*, called this dilemma "double consciousness," "a peculiar sensation...of always looking at oneself through the eyes of others." He posited that the African American "ever feels his twoness,—an American, a Negro; two souls, two thoughts, two unreconciled strivings; two warring ideals in one dark body, whose dogged strength alone keeps it from being torn asunder" (3). This objectification of oneself, to which Simone de Beauvoir referred in feminist contexts as the "Other," was, to race relations in America, like a slow-moving cancer whose destruction continues to be felt even today, in spite of the legal and social efforts of Marshall, Martin Luther King, Jr., Jesse Jackson, Louis Farrakhan, and others.

Its effect on the African American author may be much less clear; Du Bois was often ambiguous in his explanations of the concept. However, one fact is certain: Rooted explicitly among Du Bois's diverse emphases was the destructive component of internalized inferiority and personal debasement.[1] As a result, the contemporary reader must examine the concept closely to extract the constructive component Du Bois intended. Double consciousness was not, for Du Bois, the African American's destiny, but was intended instead as the cornerstone of an evolving sense of self-awareness which would pull African Americans into the American mainstream while forcing neither of the divided selves—the American nor the African—to be sacrificed. It was an important twist on an old idea. Du Bois had borrowed the term from Ralph Waldo Emerson, for whom the concept conveyed a certain fatalism, and then instilled within it an Emersonian individualism that superseded the fatalism and transformed the concept into the foundation for a more powerful African American presence in the United States. Toward that end, there is no confusion; this progressive and resourceful approach to double consciousness is clearly at the epicenter of *The Souls of Black Folk*, in spite of Du Bois's "doublespeak" in trying to define it.

In effect, African American double consciousness endowed the visible impediment of racial difference with the much more debilitating impediment of self-doubt, frustration, and anger. Nevertheless, similarly to the physical and emotional impediments that served to inspire and fuel the creativity of many of America's greatest writers—social stigmata, economic frustration, depression, addiction—the effect of racial sensitivity on African American artistic expression has been astonishing. Interwoven with the artists' desires to build a positive racial identity for black America and claim their positions as black artists in a free land, this social marginalization worked to generate a river of literary creativity and insight into the complexion, emotions, and relationships of human beings. Early admirers of African American writing were fascinated by it, though sometimes for reasons better defined by Samuel Johnson's metaphor of women preachers and dancing dogs than by genuine respect for its artistry.[2] In fact, the mere novelty of "Negro" writing was never the reason for its appeal much past the beginning of the twentieth century. For their part, black artists of all kinds had come to believe, by the 1920s, that they could earn for black America the respect it had been denied by demonstrating their mastery of the arts, and so they responded to the social circumstances by producing work that simply could not be ignored by white audiences and critics.[3]

The result of such creativity was that Du Bois's social strategy—that black America could win its share of America's rewards by besting white America at its own game—became, despite its adherence to white literary aesthetic standards, the model for black writing well into the twentieth century, and is reflected clearly in the literary style of Du Bois's contemporaries—Charles Chesnutt, Booker T. Washington, James Weldon Johnson, and Arna Bontemps, for example. Even if, as Robert Stepto argues in *From Behind the Veil* (1991), the texts of that era are now thought to be distinctively African American, they nevertheless reflected no less an attempt to reach white audiences than that of earlier African American writers—Phillis Wheatley or William Wells Brown, for example—or less sophisticated oral literature, such as "authenticated" slave narratives.[4] White audiences responded, sometimes quite enthusiastically.[5]

Quickly, the renown of black writers grew. Within a generation, by the Harlem Renaissance of the 1920s, writers like Zora Neale Hurston, Langston Hughes, Countee Cullen, Claude McKay, and Jean Toomer found considerable cross-racial success representing black America as emotionally rawer and culturally richer than did their forebears, and over time the literature changed, both stylistically and in terms of content.[6] As a result, throughout the twentieth century, the emergence of a new generation of young black writers has always seemed to signal a new stage in the evolution of African American literature—Alain Locke's new Negro in the 1920s, Zora Neale Hurston's folklore in the 1930s, Richard Wright's ideological realism in the 1940s, Ralph Ellison's philosophical complexity in the 1950s, Amiri Baraka's New Black Aesthetic in the 1960s, Toni Morrison's magical realism in the 1970s.

In the past several decades, however, literary critics, riding a wave of interest in redefining the African American literary tradition as unique and beyond interpretation or judgment by any standard other than itself, have moved toward compartmentalizing and mystifying black literature, often to the degree that the tradition came to appear as though it were but a multitude of manifestations of a single monolithic entity.[7] As a result, an operational consensus began to re-emerge among literary critics as early as the 1960s that African American literature is a homogeneous tradition, and absolutely unique in its literary properties. This Black Aesthetic movement is deeply mired in ambiguities emerging from prominent, passionate, and eloquent spokespersons who construct apologies for the existence of an "Afro-American literature," usually rooted in (without specifically saying so) the author's race and the work's racial content, but who also, frequently in the same work (though occasionally much later), insist that the literature demonstrate the same form, structure, genre, and standards of any other literary tradition. For example, Stephen Henderson writes in "The Forms of Things Unknown," his introduction to *Understanding the New Black Poetry*, that African American literature is the product of a writer of "known Black African ancestry" communicating a "commodity [known] as 'blackness,'" or the "inner life" or "interior dynamism" of African Americans, which can be "ultimately understood only by Black people themselves" (3–7); and in the same essay insists that such literature "can and should be judged by the same standards that any other poetry is judged by…" (33). Similar ambiguities exist in the works of critics as diverse as Larry Neal and Robert Stepto. Certainly, the strength of the Black Aesthetic movement is in its radical insistence that African American literature cannot be separated from its cultural roots, but many young scholars hear only the extremist rhetoric and divorce the literature from anything but the most extreme nationalist forms, sources, content, and readership, as with one student who dismissed Shelby Steele's work because, in the student's words, "he's not really black," echoing the treatment Phillis Wheatley's work has received from critics for at least forty years. Recently, such attitudes toward Afro-American essentialism have generated a backlash among many black intellectuals, including law professors Randall Kennedy (*Race, Crime, and the Law* [1997]) and Steven Carter (*Reflections of an Affirmative Action Baby* [1991]), and *Washington Post* correspondent Keith Richburg (*Out of America* [1997]).

In truth, such an isolation of literary identity is not particularly realistic, even if it were possible. Any new literary tradition must establish some synoptic identity with accepted literatures, and to do so, it must delicately balance its legitimacy among its traditional audience with the opinions of its emerging one through four distinctive channels—

- by testing its thematic and linguistic boundaries,
- by demonstrating its mastery of accepted literary forms and previous works,
- by solidifying a group self-identity through subversive appropriation of accepted forms and devices, and
- by producing works within a "shared myth" which transcend the question of their place in the established literary mainstream.

These channels, typological rather than chronological, are, for reasons related to that balance of their attitudes toward their traditional audience and their emerging one, closely related to the typology around which this work is built. That relationship will be explained when the typology itself is introduced in chapter one, and will be illustrated and explored more deeply as each of the four types is explained in greater detail in subsequent chapters. The key is this: As a result of African American authors' self-conscious and subconscious attempts to legitimize their works with a dual audience, they have, by variable degrees, written *for* the expectations of one audience and *against* those of the other audience. It is this fact upon which the thesis behind this book rests.

My goal in positing this theory is to expand the channels through which African American literature might be read and interpreted. The emerging consensus in the past generation that the African American literary tradition can be exhaustively defined by a commonality among its authors of, on the one hand, race, and on the other, ideology, has had a compressing effect on black literary criticism. The only method available to the critic who assumes that all of a field of authors are, in their essence, alike is either (1) to search for some manifestation of that similarity (usually, in the case of African American literature, grounded in figurative language, discursive style, or intertextual use of folklore) and analyze each individual work as representative of that manifestation, or (2) to filter the content of each individual work through a screen of sociological and political themes established by the critic, an exercise that inevitably discovers just the sort of commonality originally hypothesized. In some cases, the results can be intriguing. Henry Louis Gates, Jr., provides a particularly sophisticated example of the former in *The Signifying Monkey* (1988), in which the African American literary tradition is traced through a symbolic and linguistic intertextuality that has its origins in the African trickster figure and is evidenced throughout the twentieth century by the practice of "signifyin(g)," or the borrowing of linguistic components by one black author from a previous black author's work.[8] The latter method is frequently less creative, and generally seems driven by ideological intent, though its popularity in the 1960s and 1970s has inspired a generation of African American writers and critics to reject western aesthetic standards and to define Black literature in discursively unique and politically nationalistic terms. *The Black Aesthetic* (1971), edited by Addison Gayle, and *Black Fire* (1968), edited by Amiri Baraka and Larry Neal, are early well-known examples of this sociopolitical brand of criticism.

This book, though indebted to neither stream of thought, navigates terrain that bears some similarity to both, particularly at the metalinguistic, sociopsychological level. It acknowledges that writers in the African American tradition share the similarity of a dual audience, an extraliterary similarity that may or may not manifest any actual literary similitude. Similarly, it affirms the idea that social and political factors influence the thought and work of such writers, albeit in an individualized way. This approach bears some resemblance to what Houston A. Baker, Jr., calls "the poetics of integrationism" ("Generational Shifts" 3–4), in that it prioritizes an understanding that black literature emerges from a direct relationship with both the lives of black Americans and the mainstream values by which those lives are lived. In other words, a reader should never forget that to divorce the discourse of black literature from its context, black *and* white, is to risk misunderstanding it. As Bernard Bell points out in *The Afro-American Novel and Its Tradition* (1987), African American novelists are the prototypical outsiders of American society, and as a result, can utilize their dual African and western cultural heritages to construct unique visions of the human condition and its cultural context (xii).

The theory of this book is based precisely on this assumption. My point of engagement in this new perspective on double-consciousness in African American literature is with individual works as representative of the manner by which their authors negotiated the level of interaction they sought with, on the one hand, their black audience, and, on the other, their white one. At times the author has sought to meet the expectations of his or her audiences; at other times, to frustrate them. The result of such individualized and personal negotiation is a body of work as diverse as the insights its writers bring to the page. Richard Wright considers this a feature of African American society itself, writing that, "Negro life may be approached from a thousand angles with no limit to technical or stylistic freedom" ("Blueprint" 62–63). So while race may be the dominant paradigm out of which an author creates his or her vision, and may be at the core of the content and theme of the work, the black author is eminently capable of producing aesthetically significant, thematically profound literature (whether or not race is the subject) without the template of race, either in the creation of the work or in the reading of it. My own theory acknowledges such a possibility without beatifying it.

This theoretical approach, then, does not anticipate, nor even desire, that African American literature merge into some indistinguishable mainstream; to the contrary, it reads African American literature as distinctive at its very foundation. However, nothing about assuming an author to be writing out of and to a sociopsychological milieu would support the current tendency to marginalize the literature. That tendency, rooted in black nationalism and pan-Africanism, seeks a noble goal of elevating black writing in its own right, without reference to external influences or external critiques, but to divorce the literature from its western context seems as counterproductive today as it was sixty years ago, when the force behind its marginalization was white racism. Then, black literary critics Sterling Brown, Arthur P. Davis, and Ulysses Lee challenged the concept of what they called a "Negro literature" on the grounds that works by black authors could be "too easily placed by certain critics, white and Negro, in an alcove apart…[making t]he next step…a double standard of judgment…" (*The Negro Caravan* 7). That the heirs of that tradition would attempt now to place it beyond the parameters of any judgment at all, except its own, would serve the same end, and would, in the final analysis, be deeply unjust to the artists whose "double-conscious" vision of the world has created a literature distinctive in its insight and perspective and worthy of broad admiration.

What seems clear to even the casual reader is that the African American literary tradition comprises far too diverse a literary base to be represented as though it were monolithic. Contemporary black literature has experienced just the sort of gender and ideological infighting that would suggest a much more complex and anomalous tradition than is sometimes implied by critics, and the groundwork for that diversity was already in place over seventy years ago. Alain Locke, writing in 1925 in *The New Negro*, posits that, "with the Negro rapidly in process of class differentiation, if it ever was warrantable to regard and treat the Negro *en masse* it is becoming with every day less possible, more unjust and more ridiculous" (276). As black America has grown even more diverse, more educated, more class differentiated, its interaction with mainstream values has, if anything, aroused the double-consciousness of its authors to the point that, to understand the black literary tradition at all, a reader *must* place a work of literature within a sociopolitical context, including the politics of publishing and the politics of community, that has forced the African American author to write consciously for two audiences—one white, the other black—with conspicuously different goals for each. The resulting works of literature represent as broad a spectrum of values and styles as any art in American society, and are deeply integrated with it, and affirm, more than anything else, the integrity of the black author's vision of the world as an imaginative artist. That has, in one sense, always been true; African American authors have always used their double-consciousness to create literary works reflecting the tenuous personal relationships of their times, racial and social, and their perspectives on those relationships. This study explores just how their diverse attempts to approach a dual black/white audience might be categorized into a typology, based upon the differing relational depth with which the authors and their works address their constituent audiences.

The assumption that writing for different audiences would lead to different forms is not new; it is, in fact, classically dialogical. As far back as two hundred years ago, philosophers such as Johann Fichte (*The Vocation of Man* [1800]) or G.W.F. Hegel (*The Philosophy of History* [1832]) were positioning the empirical self in the context of a social world, a concept that ultimately idealized a transcendent self-awareness and the convergence of relational parties into some higher unity. Such a consideration, when applied to literary works, forces the critic to examine just how an author is so positioned; how he or she discerns and responds to the tenuous relational circumstances that "called forth" the work of art to begin with—the social dynamic that may have brought a reader to that particular work—which, of course, the writer is forced to discern even before the act of creating it. The resulting "response," the narrative or poem itself, reveals the author's interactive engagement, or, by contrast, the absence of engagement, with the readers at a transcendent relational level. For the Russian philosopher Mikhail Bakhtin, this dynamic, contrasted with its absence, creates a dichotomy between what he calls "active, responsive understanding" between author and reader and a "passive understanding that…only duplicates [an author's] own idea in someone else's head" (*Speech Genres* 86–87). As a result, any piece of literature can be evaluated, and categorized, by whether it reflects such a relational depth with an audience. This book attempts just such a categorization.

The model, as chapter 1 explains, is inspired by (and anchored within) the work of a second dialogical thinker, Jewish theologian Martin Buber (*I and Thou* [1959]). At its core, Buber's analysis dichotomizes human relationships into, on the one hand, objectified, pragmatic relationships, which he labels *I–It* and, on the other, experiential, holistic relationships, labeled *I–Thou*. The former, roughly corresponding to Bakhtin's "passive understanding," is common; the latter is elusive, emotional, and subjective, reflecting the difficulty of the "active, responsive understanding" which Bakhtin proposed. If a black author's relationship with each of his or her dual audiences (as an "ideal type") can be defined by categories resembling either *I–It* or *I–Thou*, and each of those two relationships are considered to be occurring simultaneously, then four distinct possibilities exist by which the author may interact with his or her audiences, each with a different purpose and a different philosophical foundation.[9] This is the framework for my theory. Such a categorization may seem subjective, but the subjectivity is inherent in Buber's categories of *I–Thou* and *I–It*, and is preserved in my own framework. In fact, the concept itself has literary antecedents—Hans-Georg Gadamer's hermeneutics, particularly his concept of "understanding"; or Bakhtin's metalinguistics, including his concept of heteroglossia; or the cognitive linguistic idea of "deixis," terms of address used by an author to position the reader in relation to the text.

Chapter 1 explores this theory in detail and outlines the typology devised from it. Each of four subsequent chapters examines one of the four resulting types, offering a description of each category and a close analysis for each category of one major representative work (or body of works by two similar authors) to demonstrate the author's typological approach to the challenge of double-consciousness. A final chapter posits implications of the theory for expanding our understanding of the boundaries of African American literature and its future in American letters.

To do what this book intends—that is, to refocus the criticism of African American literature away from the framework of stereotypes and toward an inquiry into the author's place and literary purpose in a social and political world (as well as a social and political industry)—is not, as some critics might suggest, a devaluation of the role of race and racial politics in shaping black writing. In fact, by choosing to address the question of race and literature, this study confronts a potential impasse with those who insist that blackness is indefatigable in its influence on the psyche, as would be inherent in Du Bois's concept of double-consciousness. Certainly, no member of an oppressed minority ever totally forgets that fact, but what this work attempts to do is recover the individuality of the black author, assuming the diversity within the tradition to be just as important as its well-explored similarities in defining its nature and place in the literary canon.

One risk, of course, is that this work might be accused of being a descent into the quagmire of "The Intentional Fallacy," a cornerstone of literary criticism for nearly seventy-five years now. However, Henry Louis Gates, Jr., has already challenged the "new critical" approach to African American literature as being, in practice, racist, and in theory, insensitive to what the race of the author would mean to the interpretation of a work ("What's Love" 347). My own theory *does* make the fundamental assumption that black authors have varying intents for their work and therefore different relationships with their dual audiences, but what those intents may be is much less important for the current analysis than the acknowledgment that the author's social, political, and literary goals result in an imaginative work with an altogether different thematic approach, style, or structure than any particular work of another type may have. In other words, my examination of *High Cotton* (1993) in Chapter 3 is not a commentary on Darryl Pinckney's intentions while writing it, but an examination of the distinctive elements of *High Cotton* that reflect Pinckney's attempts to address, in a certain and intentional way, the racial milieu in which he lives; that is, to address artistically, as well as politically, the aesthetic and thematic expectations of both a white and black audience. As Ludwig Wittgenstein has noted, "what determines our judgment, our concepts and reactions, is not what one man is doing now, an individual action, but the whole hurly-burly of human actions, the background against which we see any action" (*Zettel* 567).

What this approach does is remove the racial shorthand from African American literary criticism. Bernard Berenson, American art critic and historian, describes such shorthand in his account of the introduction of African American sculpture to Paris at the beginning of the twentieth century, a story that sounds remarkably like many contemporary efforts at defining African American literature and the influence of African American, or even African, folk traditions, discursive forms, and so on, upon it. He writes:

> When Negro sculpture first came to Paris,...the dealer...hoped to win us over by saying...that it was in the round. This cry, that Negro sculpture was in the round, you heard for a season at all the Paris dealers, and collectors, and in all Paris social gatherings, and the next season everywhere in New York, and finally...you read in luscious language in London dailies, weeklies, and monthlies, and heard at all London luncheon parties and tea-tables: "The great thing about Negro sculpture is that it is in the round." It occurred to nobody to ask..."what has their roundness to do with their being great works of art?" (795–96)

This fate could befall any art whose essential appeal is its exotic nature. For African American literature, the result is that the canon has, for many, become exotic, quaint, and set apart, intentionally or unintentionally (even as it is being anthologized more), from other literary traditions that may have influenced it, or from social or political contexts that may have inspired its very being, and would certainly influence its reception by an American literary audience. Though a reader might have any number of reasons for reading a work of African American literature, the risk of an emerging tradition becoming too quaint is that it may come to be understood as having limited appeal, as being marginalized, which is what Du Bois struggled so passionately against having done to African American literature at the beginning of the twentieth century, but which, for the past forty years or so, African American literature seems engaged at doing to itself.

My work on this subject has been motivated by a deep admiration of the emotional insight and aesthetic joy of African American literature. Of the dozens of works that come to mind when I reflect on novels and stories that have most entertained and inspired me, none of them seems important because it uses some exotic language or has some mystical connection with other works or with some mythical past. Instead, the works in this canon are the best of what most of us who have made a career of reading literature were seeking when we read our first books, and for that reason they have acquired a justified place in the literary landscape. The importance of a literary tradition does not rest in its having been created *ex nihilo*, or even that it be *sui generis*. Traditions do exist, perhaps, in a virtual vacuum, insulated from outside influence and in turn possessing only an alien influence on any culture outside its own narrow boundaries. However, the African American literary tradition is not one of these.

I hope, then, that the result of this work, would be a new generation of readers of African American literature who would become, in the words of Marcel Proust's narrator in *Remembrance of Things Past* (1924), "readers of themselves." That consistent ability of a body of literature to reflect, refine, and recreate its readers is at the core of what a literary tradition is all about. Without it, the tradition turns inward to the point of welcoming only readers who bear some biological or cultural similarity to the author. Such a literature needs no critical examination; it has already exposed its deepest flaw, and will survive only until everyone else discovers it had nothing to say to them to begin with.

Chapter 1

The Author/Audience Dialogue as Theoretical Perspective

Understanding a work of African American literature requires an understanding of the writer who composed it, or, at the very least, an understanding of the sociopolitical milieu, both interracial *and* intraracial, toward which the African American author is directing his or her art.

This requirement for understanding the sociopolitical milieu has always been applied to the African American text itself. Throughout its most productive period within America's literary history, the greater portion of the twentieth century, the black literary tradition has seen its critics continuously balance and rebalance, on the one hand, its aesthetic qualities, and on the other, its sociopolitical qualities, in an attempt to define the tradition and designate the combination of these qualities which serves to set it apart from the writing of white America. The issue inevitably becomes one of quality ("Does a novel by a black writer use some linguistic technique that one by a white writer does not?"), purpose ("Should a piece of African American writing say anything to white readers, or even be understood by them?"),[1] and their intersection at the issue of canon formation ("Is the importance of black writing for black America, or for all literary history, reason enough to require contemporary students to read it?"). The debate is important turf for both ideologues and bibliophiles, and for both, the question that seems to undergird the entire discussion is, "Does African American literature reach its highest level of actualization through aesthetic superiority with accepted forms and techniques, or by developing new devices and themes indigenous to (and by implication, specific to) its racial inimitability—by becoming, in essence, *sui generis*?" For critics like Henry Louis Gates or Houston A. Baker, the distinctive qualities of African American literature have generally leaned toward the aesthetic; for those like Maulana Ron Kerenga, Amiri Baraka, or Larry Neal, the corpus is nothing if not political. The truth is, an African American literary work is a mixture of both, and the degree and manner in which the two are mixed by an individual author reveals the author's expectations of his or her audiences and how they might read the finished work. In other words, the African American author has always engaged in the same balancing and rebalancing of the aesthetic and the sociopolitical that the critic has, weighing on the one hand how a presumed white audience might read the work, and, on the other, how a presumed black audience might read it, but for the author, the issue is creative, not just analytical.

Of course, to talk in terms of "a white audience" or "a black audience" requires a sizable amount of generalizing about such a group, and clearly risks simplifying, even caricaturing, what is in both cases a diverse and complex collective. Almost certainly, both groups would have members placed into those categories (on the basis of their racial identification, as imprecise as that may be) who would share as much in common with the other group as with their own. However, any meaningful social commentary has little choice except to talk in terms of broad similarities among members of racial groups, and fields such as sociology, cultural production theory, or African American studies clearly benefit from addressing the issue without apology or undue concern over fine distinctions of meaning.

This, then, is the premise from which I work: that African American literary efforts are rooted in both a personal and communal experience for both author and reader, and that the African American author has created his or her work with that fact in the foreground, so that interpreting any given novel or poem demands an engagement with the author's racial milieu; that is, his or her goals and expectations for a white audience as well as a black audience. Joyce A. Joyce, in "The Black Canon: Reconstructing Black American Literary Criticism" (1987), posits that a black author *must* engage a white audience with his or her unique message and language, both of which emerge from a deep investment in the human enterprise, particularly as it is experienced by black people. Even as far back as Phillis Wheatley, black authors recognized the financial and political necessity of reaching a white audience. Analyzing the literary result, then, becomes an attempt to unpackage the author's social and aesthetic forms and content from a single bundle given to two strikingly different audiences at the same time. Joyce suggests the importance of just such an analysis when she writes that "The job of the…literary critic should be to find a point of merger between the communal, utilitarian, phenomenal nature of Black literature and the aesthetic or linguistic—if you will—analyses that illuminate the 'universality' of the literary text" (337). To challenge the African American reader with the implications of the author's having had that second, white, audience is, she says, an "act of love." The critic of African American literature, free to go where the writer cannot, should "force ideas to the surface…in order to affect, to guide, to animate, and to arouse the minds and emotions of Black people" (342). It is this intersection between author and audience that is at the core of dialogical thought, so that understanding this dialogic becomes the nerve center for reading African American literature.

Contemporary African American literary criticism has, at least tacitly, acknowledged this dialogic. For Henry Louis Gates, in *The Signifying Monkey*, this contextual dialogue between reader and author of African American writing is at the core of what he believes to be distinctive about African American literature—the use by the African American author of what philosopher Mikhail Bakhtin called "double-voiced discourse," creating what can be called a hidden polemic. By "double-voicing," Bakhtin means an utterance that embodies both the speaker's point of view and a second speaker's simultaneous evaluation of that utterance, decolonized for black purposes, according to Gates, "by inserting a new semantic orientation into a word which already has—and retains—its own orientation" (50). Black writers regularly use this technique, Gates posits, in a self-referential intertextuality of the black text that he calls "Signifyin(g)," or the conscious appropriation and iteration, often in a playful manner, of previous literary forms and styles into a new context.

For Dorothy J. Hale, the concept of double-voicing is a bit more problematic, particularly among those critics who equate it, in African

American literature, with Du Bois's concept of "double-consciousness." Hale posits that Du Bois is misunderstood by critics who tend to interpret his ambiguous explanations of double-consciousness through the lens of Bakhtinian heteroglossia, ultimately conflating them. By contrast, she sees the two concepts—"double-voicing" and "double-consciousness"—as antithetical. Double-consciousness, she explains, is a socially constructed model of subordination; double-voicing a unilateral seizure of social power through the use of "the authentic de-essentialized self, made manifest." Taken together, she writes, they allow the critic "to transform the Du Boisian crisis of subaltern invisibility into a Bakhtinian triumph of self-articulation" (201). In spite of what may be an overly negative and depreciating opinion of Du Bois's concept, Hale opens the door for its consonance with Bakhtin's theory when she argues that what ultimately attracts critics to the idea of merging the two concepts is the emphasis in both on the socially constructed subject (214). The *double-conscious* African American author possesses what Hale suggests is "a privileged kind of knowledge," the ability to see and experience both hegemonic power and otherness, "Americanness" and "blackness," and the *double-voiced* African American author has the ability to put those complexities into a character's words, or two characters' words, each with conflicting perspectives on the dialogue. Using both, the African American author can vacillate among a polyphony of familiar voices in a heteroglossic work so complex that, given the dual audience for which African American authors write, the work itself may be read differently by its different audiences.

The role of the reader, then, can never be divorced from the African American author's construction of the text. Bakhtin believed that a writer's unique act of expression, "an expression of the position of someone speaking individually in a concrete situation of speech communication" (*Speech Genres* 84), emerges as the product of an internal dialogue in which the voices of others, past and present, are integrated with one's own voice to create, "speech...filled to overflowing with other people's words" (*Dialogic Imagination* 337). In effect, the act of writing or speaking cannot be divorced from its social construction, both in its origins as a dialogue with the author's past and present context, as well as in its reception by an audience, or dual audiences, bringing to the present dialogue their own historical and contextual interaction. As Bakhtin notes, "any understanding is imbued with response and necessarily elicits it in one form or another: the listener becomes the speaker" (*Speech Genres* 68). The reader receives a text as if engaging in a dialogue, and the response that emerges is framed by the ongoing dialogue in which the text and reader are engaged; to interpret a text one way will elicit one response, to interpret it another elicits a different response, and because, as Robert Frost reminds us, "way leads on to way," just how a reader constructs the dialogue he or she shares with a text at any given moment makes, one could say, "all the difference." That a white reader might construct that dialogue differently from a black reader is patently obvious.

However, interpreting a work of literature by an African American writer is not primarily an issue of reader response; Bakhtin is insistent that discourse cannot be separated from the person speaking it ("Discourse" 262–70). Even so, he is equally insistent that it cannot be separated from the person receiving it (Voloshinov 85–86). It lies in a place Martin Buber calls the "between," or as Bakhtin calls it, "a bridge thrown between myself and another" (*Speech Genres* 86). To privilege either the author or, and perhaps especially, the reader would be to overlook the dynamic that ultimately creates the work, even in the cross-racial context of African American literature. An author has precisely the same sort of dialogue with a text as a reader does, and for the author, the context in which he or she reads his or her own textual utterance (even before it is written) is the ongoing dialogue that the reader, at some point in the future, will be having with it. The result, the Bakhtinian Circle suggests, is that contextuality serves to privilege the practice of intonation, in an attempt to secure the meaning of the utterance without sacrificing its intercontextuality (Medvedev 133–44). To examine the text for evidence of such intonation would generally be fruitless, as any textual traces of it are indiscernible, but as an approach by which to suggest that an author posits a tentative monologism (more or less, depending on the author and his or her attempts to engage a black audience as opposed to, or in harmony with, a white one) with the complete expectation that the reader will be engaging the utterance in a contextually driven dialogue, it offers interesting new insights into the double-conscious and potentially double-voiced narrative of the African American text. In other words, in spite of the fact that a critic (or reader, for that matter) may not see any evidence of an African American author's attempt to secure the meaning of his or her text, the attempt was nevertheless made, and presumably can be inferred by the critic.

Even more importantly for this present approach, the critic must remember that the reader, as one might use the term to refer to an actual reader, really has nothing at all to do with how a work of African American literature might be interpreted (apart from the dialogue that the author and text have with the reader). From the perspective of the text itself—that is, its compositional creation as one side of a dialogue—the key moment in the dialogue is the author's response to the presumed reader at the point of creation (which shapes the nature of the utterance itself), not the actual response of any particular reader, which, though part of the dialogue which authentically shapes the text's meaning as an utterance, is engaged in a dialogical moment separate from and subsequent to the creative compositional work of the author.[2] In spite of Paul de Man's assertion that a reader eventually reaches a point when no amount of textual analysis can help him/her evade the "fearful symmetry" of engagement and ambiguity (*Resistance* 15–17), the reader learns nothing about an utterance and the voice behind it—a piece of literature and its author—from a misinformed or ideological misreading of it, regardless of the resulting level of engagement or dialogue. A critic might further assume that the richer a text's allusions and the more complex its thematic rendering, the more likely such misreadings would occur. With the resulting transfer of materiality from the text to the product of interpretation, the dialogue between text and reader becomes wholly dependent upon context. As Seymour Chatman writes, "...*mere* reading is not an aesthetic experience....The perceiver must at some point mentally construct the 'field' or 'world' of the aesthetic object" (27). For the study of a body of literature dependent upon a distinguishing social or personal characteristic in its "authors"—ethnic literature, feminist literature, gay literature, and so forth—actual reader response, the "field" constructed by any specific person (open to an infinite number of contextualized readings), is irrelevant, even when it appears to be addressing the author in a sort of timeless dialectic.

Consider the critical response to Ralph Ellison's *Invisible Man* (1952) by the "Black Aesthetic" critic Larry Neal. In 1968, when the ashes of Watts and Detroit were rekindling in the wake of Martin Luther King's assassination, Neal sarcastically wrote that, in contrast to Ellison's invisible man, "we know who we are, and are not invisible, at least not to each other. We are not Kafkaesque creatures stumbling through a white light of confusion and absurdity" ("Shine" 652). However, by 1987, Neal had reconsidered his earlier assault on the novel, praising it unreservedly as a complex and ironic portrayal of African American life, attitudes, and artistry ("Zoot Suit" 105–24). Clearly, Neal himself had changed in the twenty-year interval between 1968 and 1987; his maturation as a literary critic and the mellowing of his attitude and rhetoric seem familiar to all of us. Certainly the times changed. The book itself, though, did not change; it remained throughout the period, and remains today, a record of Ellison's creative act, his dialogue with the black and white audience for whom the novel was written. Certainly, an analysis of one reader's evolution of opinion about a novel or poem, or of radically different readings of a text by two concurrent readers, offers the possibility of fresh and revealing insights about the text as a historical relic, or even a literary relic. What it says, however, about the text as a manuscript sitting in its author's typewriter or still in its author's head is negligible; Ellison could not have been dialogically engaged with every conceivable response to his novel.

However, for whatever irrelevance a specific reader's response may have for the creation of the work, the reader is nonetheless crucial in establishing a community of peers with which the African American author considers himself, at the point of creation, in dialogue—that is, the author may ordinarily be presumed to write for a "race-conscious literati," both white and black, not to any abstract population of all whites and all blacks. It is the community whose voices the author has assimilated to form his or her own voice, and the community to whom the author speaks through the externalized discourse of the novel or poem, and it is at the intersection of the author's intent for that work and the reader's response to it, preempted and inculcated by the author, that the work itself is created. Specifically, in the inculcation of "otherness," the author comes to know his or her characters (and why they behave as they do), his or her readers, both black and white, and ultimately, himself or herself.

Bakhtin posited this idea before more completely developing the concept of dialogics, and in an interesting coincidence, outlined the process (without using such terminology) in terms of the author developing a "double-consciousness"—one shaped through the experience of the "other," the second through the consummation of that experience in terms of ourselves. For the African American author, for whom this theory seems naturally to fit, the white community to whom he or she writes, or perhaps more accurately, the white community to whom the author *perceives* himself or herself to be writing, transforms the author's self-identity as a "universal" author; the perceived black community to whom he or she writes serves the same consummating function for the author's experience as "universal" author in terms of his or her self-image as an African American author. In that sense, the author escapes being just a black writer for a black community. Toni Morrison understands this dynamic well, having Sethe say to herself in *Beloved* (1987), "Freeing yourself was one thing. Claiming ownership of that freed self was another" (95).

To engage both a white audience and a black audience in such a self-consummating way requires an authentic voice and consciousness for each, a manifestation of what Bakhtin called "polyphony," or the device wherein an author creates characters whose consciousnesses adhere to and posit distinctively different ideologies from the author (*Problems* 20). Fyodor Dostoevsky, Bakhtin believed, was the first author to achieve this dynamic; Leo Tolstoy, its antithesis. In contrast to monological writers like Tolstoy, who presume to "possess a ready-made truth," either through naivete or ideological overconfidence, dialogical writers employ polyphonic methods to *engage* "the truth" (110). Such truth, Bakhtin writes, "is not born nor is it found inside the head of an individual person; it is born between people collectively searching for truth, in the process of their dialogic interaction" (110).

Bakhtin does not propose that an author writes from some theoretical world of abstract unity, where final, authoritative interpretations of texts exist to be decoded through some exercise of common logic (Roberts 133–34). Bakhtin, one must remember, wrote in an age of formalism, sometimes as a critic of that movement, and so readily acknowledges the vagueness and ambiguity of texts. In fact, it is precisely that ambiguity which offers both reader and author the role of creating meaning through socially derived and linguistically shared readings, or in other words, dialogically. He writes that to live is to participate in dialogue: "to ask questions, to heed, to respond, to agree" (*Problems* 293).

For the African American author, this creative task is heightened by the presence of a dual reader with which the author conducts his dialogical enterprise. This would imply, of course, a complex three-way dialogue—author, white audience, and black audience (even if the dialogue were intended to exclude one of its parties)—which could forever place the author, and would certainly place the critic of the resulting text, in the impossible circumstance of guessing just how such chaos might be sorted out. However, this seems to be precisely what Bakhtin had in mind. For any author who seeks genuine dialogue in the truth-seeking sense in which Bakhtin sometimes used the term, the polyphonic presence of a plurality of voices, all free to contradict the author, is an essential element. As James Thomas Zebroski points out, "Bakhtin suggests that such conflict is natural, even inevitable, and that we need to accept such dialogue or quarrel as a starting point since real coherence in a text may come about less because the many voices have been suppressed and silenced, than because they have become dialogic, speaking with, even at times yelling at, each other and the 'writer' who is made up of this community of voices" (232). That the African American author must confront the plurality of voices more intentionally, and with greater effort, only heightens the opportunity for polyphony, and offers the possibility of bridging the gap between the novel's aesthetic elements and its sociopolitical elements—or in Bakhtin's words, between art and life.[3]

Nevertheless, the African American author's approach to his or her dual audience is a tricky undertaking, and the critic of the resulting work must ultimately be as willing as the author to suspend societal and critical expectations placed on such a work of literature, its author, and ultimately its critic. Both Black America and White America, each with its distinctive way of thinking about and experiencing race, have developed their own more or less comprehensive and coherent *Weltanschauungen*. Perspective, though, is not prescription. To step outside such a system in the dialogic of authorship does not require a black author to abandon his or her convictions about race, or his or her identification with a traditional racial group; neither should it require the critic to overlook the influence of the "Other." If anything, Bakhtin's dialogic makes clear that language, particularly polyphonic language (as would be inherent in a double-voiced, double-conscious African American novel), is saturated with the words of others, and that the task of creating—and interpreting—a text is to orchestrate the symphony of voices into some meaningful textual unity.

The key to interpreting the African American author's double-conscious dialogic, then, seems to reside in understanding, or at least making inferences about, how the author has engaged this symphony in creating his or her literary work. At this point, Martin Buber is clear: in order to construct this chorus, the black author must confront the reality of the genuine dialogical situation with both the black "Other" and the white "Other" for whom he or she writes, and either engage, or refuse to engage, that "Other" in a dialogue best characterized by a *hypostasis*, or perfect knowledge, unencumbered by any "system of ideas,…foreknowledge, and…fancy" (*I and Thou* 11). Such a literature will inevitably seem to peer right into the soul of a reader. The alternative, or what we might term a refusal to engage the Other with this degree of intensity, would leave the writer only the option of literary *pragmatism*, an engagement of the reader at the level of consequences, or social reality, resulting in a literature saturated with "ideas, foreknowledge, and fancy," and at its most extreme, monologic in its voice. Neither of these approaches should have any value attached, because they do not represent at the analytical level, or even at the aesthetic level, success or failure by an individual author, only a reflection of the author's intent in the creation of the work. The concepts, "hypostasis" and "pragmatism," are intended in this context to mean roughly what the dictionary says they mean, but given the abstract nature of their use in the context of this theory, especially as they would manifest themselves in a given literary work, the following lists may be helpful in understanding the literary application.

Hypostasis	*Pragmatism*
• mutual encounter	• detached observation
• experiential	• didactic
• ontological engagement	• intellectual engagement
• self-awareness	• objective apperception
• dialogical	• monological
• literary expression	• extraliterary expression
• racial engagement	• racial identification
• naturalistic	• idealistic

The engagement of the reader at the hypostatic level pushes the author to a higher (or perhaps deeper), more complex level of discourse with the reader, one that may be loosely called, in Bakhtinian terms, "polyphony"; in Buberian terms, "I-Thou." In addition, such a work would, for both these dialogical theorists, represent an ideal. "This," Buber writes, "is the eternal source of art: a man is faced by a form which desires to be made through him into a work" (9). For both of them, it is the act of engagement that completes the literary task, but such engagement is never assured. Buber writes:

> the primary word can only be spoken with the whole being. He who gives himself to it may withhold nothing of himself. The work does not suffer me, as do the tree and the man, to turn aside and relax in the world of *It*; but it commands. If I do not serve it aright it is broken, or it breaks me. (10)

For an author to engage a *dual* audience in such a way seems Herculean. How much more difficult, then, is the critic's task of discerning (or at least inferring) the African American author's engagement of that dual audience, temporalized and objectified by the racial politics deeply ingrained in a social context? This much is clear: The African American author must engage both audiences, and may address either audience at the hypostatic level or at the pragmatic level. As a result, the interlacing of potential dual approaches to a dual audience makes certain that African American literature will include a distinctively variegated body of works, differentiated in either substance or form, or both, specific to the approach the author takes toward his or her dual audience. At the same time, however, the admixture of contrasting audiences also suggests strongly that the resulting arabesque can, in fact, be reduced to a quaternary typology into which African American literary works will necessarily fall, and through which those works can be critiqued, compared, and evaluated. If both white audience and black audience are placed separately on an axis so that the intersection of an African American author's approach to both audiences can be charted, and the author's level of engagement with each audience—either hypostatic or pragmatic—identified and crosscut with his or her level of engagement with the other audience, the result can be diagramed in the manner illustrated in Figure 1.

This dialogical approach allows a critic to posit three tentative assumptions. It appears not only possible but logical that an African American writer could position himself or herself to address two audiences at once—one black, the other white—with the same literary work. Second, the differentiation among the four categories seems clear enough to suggest not only that African American writers occupy one of four distinct authorial positions, but also that the result of such diverse authorial approaches would be four manifestly different literary products. Finally, the graphic seems to reveal not only a *variance* of authorial positions, and as a result, literary types, but an *antithesis* of types between those literatures represented by opposing corners of the chart. Specifically, one opposing pair would represent contrasting ways that both audiences may be addressed similarly by the author; the other opposing pair, contrasting ways in which the two audiences may be addressed differently.

Figure 1: Author/Reader Relational Matrix

		Black	Reader
		Pragmatic	*Hypostatic*
White	*Pragmatic*		
Reader	*Hypostatic*		

The key to the African American author's ability to stand at this intersection of two dialogues at once, turning them into a single literary work (though not a unitary language, which Bakhtin insisted could not exist), lies in that author's expectation that the work will be perfectly understood as an accurate reflection of his or her racial self-concept; in other words, that a perfectly understanding mediator is reading over his or her shoulder. That seemingly acrobatic act of writing is given shape and meaning in that intangible, but very real, space between author and audience, a realm Martin Buber called, in his relational theology, the "between" (*Between* 9). Buber writes:

> what is essential does not take place in each of the participants or in a neutral world which includes the two and all other things; but it takes place between them in the most precise sense, as if it were in a dimension which is accessible only to them both....On the far side of the subjective, on this side of the objective, on a narrow ridge, where I and Thou meet, there is the realm of the "between." (203–4)

It is in this "between," or rather the dual "betweens" of dual audiences, that my own theory finds its direction, not only because of Buber's social, even ontological, vision of the dialogical nature of literary creation, but because, as the Bakhtin Circle points out in *Marxism and the Philosophy of Language* (Voloshinov [1930]), every text defines its author in relation to its reader, and its reader in relation to its author (65). In effect, the "between" is the point at which the meeting of author and reader finds its true essence. The result, of course, is that the critic comes to understand the author, the reader, and ultimately the text through such an understanding of the dynamic exemplified by the "between."

This attention to the context of the utterance (or in the case of a writer, the text itself) is unmistakable in Bakhtin's work, and features two components which play significant roles in this theory—the concept of "addressivity," or an awareness of the otherness of dialogic partners, and the concept of "answerability," the investment of axiological value in a relational other through our own tentative engagement with our creative endeavors. The former leads Bakhtin to posit a "superaddressee," an objective (but abstract) manifestation of Buber's "between" who, in this present theory, might be understood to represent an African American author's idealized intent for the reception of his or her text by a specific racially identified audience. The latter offers an umbrella under which an African American author's literary and social distance from that specific audience might be posited.

There, in the idea of the superaddressee, Bakhtin outlines a concept whereby the African American author can write with, and can be assumed by the critic to have written with, the confidence that his literary endeavor—its intentions, its content, and its themes—will be understood by both black and white audiences, or rather, by an "ideal" of each audience and both audiences simultaneously. It is, for Bakhtin, a higher authority (though not necessarily an anthropomorphic one) which the author addresses beyond, and in addition to, the presumed reader. The key is that the superaddressee is presumed by the author to possess an "absolutely just responsive understanding… , either in some metaphysical distance or in historical time (the loophole addressee)" (*Speech Genres* 126).

The only way, therefore, for a critic to begin to piece together some meaning from the double-voiced, double-conscious (even dualistic) model of African American literary production is to move into the "between" to find that third presence, the superaddressee, and integrate that presence into the dialogic. This superaddressee is not, Bakhtin suggests, any sort of third partner in dialogue; in fact, it was for Bakhtin a generalized enough concept to be "God, absolute truth, the court of dispassionate human conscience, the people, the court of history, science" (*Speech Genres* 126). As such, its presence does not disturb the dualistic model of the dialogical situation confronting the African American author. Because of its "absolutely just responsive understanding," it must instead be construed as existing always in unity with the author and the author's intent in his or her dialogical relationship with both of his or her dual audiences, both independently and as a structural unity to which the singular communication that is the novel is addressed. The aim is not to emphasize critical understandings and misunderstandings of the author's utterances, but is instead designed to affirm as a critical starting point that in some ideal place in the hermeneutic circle, the African American author was able to create a work that has communicated what he or she had hoped to say to a white audience, and what he or she had hoped to say to a black audience. The role of the superaddressee is to overhear the utterance, so to speak, and offer the author, at the point of creation, a perspective that the novel is an utterance for the ages. It is that utterance which the critic seeks.

One potential approach to this endeavor, and a fraudulent one for Bakhtin, is for the author to place himself or herself into the role of the "Other," seeking to view and produce his or her work not from the position of a reader—black or white—but from the position of some generalized "indeterminate potential other" ("Author and Hero" 31), an abstract other with no specific characteristics at all. Bakhtin calls an author who attempts such an exercise a "pretender," equating his or her actions to a contract without a signature, "obligating no one and obliged to nothing" (Morson and Emerson, *Prosaics* 180–81). For Bakhtin, taking someone else's place is an even worse strategy for establishing dialogue than simply staying in one's own place, for the result of such an attempt is to make the author a "soul-slave," confusing an I-for-others with an I-for-myself. An author focusing on himself or herself can only *impersonate* an "other," Bakhtin says, and regardless of the success an author may have doing such an impersonation, he or she would still only have a sense of myself-for-others, a very different thing from the I-for-myself (Morson and Emerson, *Prosaics* 181). In effect, Bakhtin makes clear that a text remains richer and more complete with the presence of a clearly distinct other, asking rhetorically: "In what way would it enrich the event if I merged with the other, and instead of two there would be now only one? And what would I myself gain by the other's merging with me? If he did,…he would merely repeat in himself that want of any issue out of itself which characterizes my own life. Let him rather remain outside of me…" (*Art* 87).

In the concept of the "soul-slave," even beyond Bakhtin's ironic and uncomfortable reference to enslavement, lies an important dialogical truth: An African American author cannot, with integrity or aesthetic success, imagine himself or herself in the place of a reader, especially given the double-conscious task of having a dual, socially (and perhaps aesthetically) contrasting audience. Because, then, it is not an "Other," but an authentic reader, white or black, who completes the dialogical circle, a critic must resist the temptation to specify what a text might be saying to a "black audience" or a "white audience." This sort of identification with a specific reader has no place in my theory, even though it may, at times, seem to be the purpose of my theoretical approach. Bakhtin is adamant that it is impossible to infer from features in the text itself what has been constructed between the author (through the text) and the reader; that is a unique social transaction (*Dialogic Imagination* 292). What *is* important is the attempt by the critic to come to some understanding that a particular text has been constructed by its author with a confidence that its superaddressee would correctly interpret its relational approach with both its black audience and its white audience.

In order to represent an "ideally true responsive understanding" of the African American author's intent for the work, the superaddressee must reflect the writer's understanding of how an African American author would, in an ideal literary dialogic, position himself or herself with his or her dual audience, certainly with each individually, but more importantly, given the indivisible, even if not especially univocal, nature of a text, as one entity engaged in a dialogic with both simultaneously. Cornell West, in an essay encompassing over a hundred years of debate about the African American artist's best access to America's literary and social economy (and almost confessionally emerging from his own position as black author), supports the idea that African American authors stake out one of four authorial positions, rooted primarily in their own personal choices regarding their approach to their dual white and black audiences. West never explicitly defines his types in such dialogical terms, but because of the necessity, West posits, for African American authors to balance self-confidence and perseverance (presumably through *consentaneity* with a white audience and white literary values) with a measure of *independence* from mainstream approval, they are forced to choose one of four options for their creative work (25–27). The first, which he pejoratively calls the "Booker T. Temptation," is the attempt by the black author to position himself or herself in the political and social position to succeed within the mainstream, and on the basis of those mainstream values. The approach, West writes, tends to lead to a "pervasive professionalism," or what may be considered a writer's faculty for engaging his or her white patrons, but the result, West makes clear, is the disintegration of the writer's own "work,…outlook and, most important,…soul" (26). As the present theory will demonstrate, the black writer's method of remaining connected to the African American tradition is to use such literary professionalism in a subversive manner. The result, however, is that even the most talented of such writers tend to remain marginalized.

The second, what West calls the "Talented Tenth Seduction," is the "arrogant" move by a black author into the mainstream as an unusually gifted African American writer. Such an approach, West suggests, reinforces racialist attitudes about the writer's work by self-consciously raising the specter of race among the white mainstream while "insulating" the work from its larger black constituency. As my own theory demonstrates, however, the resulting work actually takes on a mythological quality for both audiences. The effect, for the successful author, is that even as he or she comes to be identified with black identity and black themes, both black and white readers admire, even revere, the quality of the work.

A third option, to "Go It Alone," rejects the mainstream in, as West defines it, an intellectually limiting attempt at creative independence, presumably focusing on African American themes and forms. West implies what my own theory posits: that such an author understands the complex politics of writing for a dual audience, and sees creative independence as an asset to be seized, so he or she prioritizes the political message of social and literary inversion—black over white. However, what the approach gains initially in creative energy, West writes, is soon lost amid the isolation inherent in such an approach.

The final option, and for West, the most viable one, is for the author to be what he calls a "Critical Organic Catalyst." What West describes in such a "catalyst" is the somewhat idealized (though not unattainable) African American author who masters mainstream forms and values while remaining clearly identified with his or her cultural and racial heritage. Such an approach, West writes, demonstrates "openness to…the mainstream" without "wholesale cooptation, and group autonomy" without "group insularity" (27). West identifies only a handful of high-achieving models of this type—Martin Luther King, Jr., W.E.B. Du Bois, Louis Armstrong, and Wynton Marsalis.

For West, all four options are highly politicized, and he describes the first three with considerable disdain, but when analyzed more objectively, free of the political baggage West attaches, the four options he describes bear a remarkable similarity to the four categories in the typology above, and serve to legitimate it.[4] In fact, what the categories suggest is not only an approach a black writer might consciously take toward his or her dual audiences, but also an idealized reading of the work, such as might be tendered by the writer's superaddressee. Placing each of West's categories into the schemata above begins to produce a clearer image of how this typology might look, as illustrated in Figure 2.

His "Booker T. Temptation," given its author's keen awareness of his or her white audience and the work's emotional distance from its black audience, reflects one distinct example of the authorial relationship with that author's dual audience (or perhaps more precisely, his or her superaddressee), and suggests an approach that would stand in direct contrast to West's concept of "Going It Alone," which, as the name implies, describes an African American author's direct and holistic relationship with his or her black audience and an indirect, instrumental approach to the mainstream white audience. The "Booker T. Temptation," as the name implies, appears to the less sophisticated reader to be a bad faith rejection by an African American author of his or her own racial heritage, and as such, West's implication in choosing such a name would be misleading in the context of my own theory. Instead, as suggested earlier, the theoretical implication of such an authorial position in my own theory would be an ideology of subversion, an undercutting of social and literary convention by appealing directly and skillfully to its expectations, then subverting them—linguistically, structurally, or thematically. It is a familiar social position for black America, and a literary position that allows an African American author, in the words of Jack-the-Bear's grandfather in Ralph Ellison's *Invisible Man* (1952), to "overcome 'em with yeses, undermine 'em with grins, agree 'em to death and destruction" (18). By contrast, "Going It Alone" is rooted in an ideology of subordination, and seeks to challenge social and literary convention by rejecting its expectations. The result is a literature that often demonstrates its author's independent spirit through provocative challenges to mainstream white assumptions and values.

The "Talented Tenth Seduction," as West describes it, implies a certain utilitarian approach to both audiences, to a large degree resulting from the intellectual isolation such a "talented" African American author experiences from his or her audiences, which results in a literature that seems to both white and black audiences to be driven by, to use Buber's words, "ideas, foreknowledge, and fancy." Quite likely, the result often even feels, to both audiences, monological, or as they might call it, "authoritative" or "mythic." Such a literature, or superaddressee, or authorial relational position (each would, in some ways, be an accurate term here) would stand in clear contrast to a literature (or authorial position or superaddressee) that conveyed to both audiences a perfect knowledge of their psycho-social milieus, their lives, their "souls." The latter, in fact, might even feel to the reader, among both audiences, like the author had taken a journey of discovery in racial America and they had come along for the ride. The paradox is clear; the literature that seeks to peer most deeply into its reader's marrow, into his or her *hypostasis*, nonetheless seems, because of its depth of character, of time and place and action, more verisimilar than the literature which engages both audiences at the pragmatic, or consequential, level, the one produced with a "talented tenth" sensibility. Such a "pragmatic" literature, because of its depth of ideas, its origins in an author who is both patrician and plebeian, its appeal to eternal truths (indeed, even its illumination of such truths), seems idealistic, fabulistic, and pious in its quest for an African American "tradition."

Figure 2: Author/Reader Relational Matrix

		Black	Reader
		Pragmatic	*Hypostatic*
White Reader	*Pragmatic*	The "Talented Tenth" Seduction	Going It Alone
	Hypostatic	The Booker T. Temptation	The Critical Organic Catalyst

The result, then, is a schematic which not only defines an author's simultaneous relationship with his or her dual audience (through the mediation of the superaddressee), but also differentiates a resulting type of literature—four literary types in all—characterized by that relational position, or perhaps more accurately, by the superaddressee who would "respect" the relational turf staked out by the author. The resulting typology, illustrated in Figure 3, defines the starting point for my critical approach to African American fiction.

Because two of these types result from an author's identical relational position with both black audiences and white audiences—in one case, hypostasis; in the other, pragmatism—those works each clearly represent what may be called an "ideal type" of author-audience interaction. As a result, each is best identified by a name which describes its treatment of the African American milieu: *mythification* for the idealistic, didactic, monologistic literature devoted to the saga, the legend, the myth of African American life in America; *vivification* for the naturalistic, experiential, dialogical literature focused on a portrayal of the essentiality, the complex reality, of African American life.

Figure 3: Author/Reader Relational Matrix

		Black Reader	
		Pragmatic	*Hypostatic*
White Reader	*Pragmatic*	Literature Of Mythification	Literature Of Inversion
	Hypostatic	Literature Of Subversion	Literature Of Vivification

The other two types acquire their distinctiveness from the fact that the author occupies antithetical relational positions with his or her white audience and black audience. In such a situation, an African American author may engage black readers both racially and ontologically in a mutual and dialogical exploration of the black experience, leaving white readers to dismiss it, or be insulted by it or perplexed by it, as a didactic, idealistic, and ultimately fantastical portrayal of race in America. To accomplish this would clearly be an *inversion* of not only the expectations of a white audience for the story, but its political and emotional ability to control the text itself. Or the author may do the opposite, engaging white readers and confounding black readers, but undertake it as a method of *subversion* of the very aspects of the work that would seem so pleasurable, and authentic, to the white reader.

One additional component of this typology is that, as a result of its analysis of an African American author's relational approach to his or her dual audience, it also positions itself as a typology by which a new literary tradition might balance its legitimacy with its traditional and natural audience against that with its emerging audience. As outlined earlier, such a balance requires four equally important functions:

- the testing of boundaries by which the new tradition might operate before alienating or angering the literary establishment it seeks to join,
- the demonstration of its mastery of accepted literary forms and previous traditions,
- the solidification of a "group self-identity" for and with its natural audience through subversive appropriation of accepted forms and devices,
- the production of a "shared mythology" among both audiences which transcends the question of the literary work's place in the established literary mainstream.

Remarkably, the four literary types which have emerged in this study each serve logically and naturally one of these functions. The Literature of Inversion will, by virtue of its nature, test established boundaries by challenging the literary mainstream's self-awareness and understanding of previously excluded cultural groups and literary forms. The Literature of Vivification utilizes generally accepted canons and forms in impressive ways to explore and present subject matter unique to the culture of the emerging tradition. The Literature of Subversion is characterized precisely because it appropriates those accepted forms and canons in ways that confound and subvert the establishment with subtle linguistic and political undercurrents. The Literature of Mythification transcends the issues it appears to be addressing and creates an authoritative mythology through which the emerging tradition and the established tradition come together to project a common literary future. As a result, not only are each of these four literary types *descriptive* of an emerging literature, they are also essential to and *prescriptive* for a successful transition of new forms and themes from being marginalized literary oddities to becoming an established literary tradition.

Subsequent chapters in this work will explore the literary types in detail, but a brief example may demonstrate here how the typology might define literary differences even among works by the same author, in this case, Zora Neale Hurston.[5] Because of their brevity, these illustrations are little more than "paintbrush sketches" of either the literary works from which they draw or the literary type they represent. Inasmuch as the purpose of the subsequent chapters is to explore these literary types more extensively, my goal in these examples from Hurston has been merely to demonstrate the viability of the model and whet an interest in further examination.

Barbara Johnson, in the essay "Thresholds of Difference: Structures of Address in Zora Neale Hurston," points out a remarkable contrariety in two of Hurston's best known essays, a contrariety based largely on Hurston's expectation that one of the essays is addressed primarily to a white audience, the other to a black audience. The result is not just contrasting ideas, which Johnson explores in marvelous detail, but contrasting types of literature, driven by Hurston's rebalancing of her authorial position as it would relate with each of her dual audiences (317). The essays "How It Feels to Be Colored Me" (1928) and "What White Publishers Won't Print" (1950) both foreground race as the issue under consideration, and both eventually arrive at what would have been a common black stereotype during Hurston's life—the Negro as primitive African savage. But how she handles them, as Johnson points out, demonstrates distinctly different authorial positions (321–22). For example, at a crucial point in "How It Feels to Be Colored Me," Hurston tells her dual audience about listening to a jazz orchestra with a white friend with whom she already feels little in common. As the orchestra begins playing one number with a particularly "rambunctious...primitive fury," she reports feeling drawn toward "the jungle": "I dance wildly inside myself; I yell within, I whoop; I shake my assegai above my head, I hurl it true to the mark yeeeeooww! I am in the jungle and living in the jungle way. My face is painted red and yellow and my body is painted blue. My pulse is throbbing like a war drum. I want to slaughter something—give pain, give death to what, I do not know" (154). Too soon, the music ends, and she returns to "the veneer we call civilization" to find her friend completely unmoved, tapping the beat on the tabletop. "Good music they have here," is all he can say, and at that point, Hurston notices just how distant are his heritage and hers: "He is so pale with his whiteness then and I am so colored."

This is evidence of what I call "The Literature of Subversion." The white reader is approached in this essay hypostatically, primarily as voyeur; the black reader more pragmatically, idealistically (evidenced by her sarcastic opening line, "I am colored but I offer nothing in the way of extenuating circumstances except the fact that I am the only Negro in the United States whose grandfather on the mother's side was *not* an Indian chief"). As a result, she seems to be deferring to a 1930s white audience's expectations about the African savage inherent in the Negro personality, but manages clearly and successfully to undermine those expectations by portraying an archetypal white character who is so unmoved by the music that he may be assumed to be dead ("so pale with his whiteness"). Further analysis of this essay would continue to demonstrate Hurston's masterful use of subversion as a literary type—dancing and singing for gullible white tourists intertwined with frank discussion about racial identity that would have the effect of elevating black pride while undercutting white stereotypes.

Devoid of much of the humor that characterized "How It Feels to Be Colored Me," a tone that seduced a white audience before catching them in its thematic trap, the 1950 essay "What White Publishers Won't Print" immediately stakes out the high ground in a more serious, some might say more sober, discussion about racial stereotypes. From her confrontational title to her casual disregard for a white audience, Hurston produces a classic example of "The Literature of Inversion," a literature that seems unambiguously to convey the majority culture as "type"—narrow-minded and, even worse perhaps, simple-minded, falling far short of a cultured and insightful black America. The essay itself works as a subtle example of her argument, positing that white America fears the revelation of its sameness with black America, written in an erudite language that conveys such complexity of thought as to almost obscure the argument, as in the following: "As long as the majority cannot conceive of a Negro…feeling and reacting inside just as they do, the majority will keep right on believing that people who do not feel like them cannot possibly feel as they do" (171). The effect, of course, is to make the white reader a stranger in his or her own arena, the arena of language and logic, while conveying a refinement, even an elegance, among and toward the essay's clearly implied audience—black readers.

The critical and popular success of Hurston's longer works indicate an even more profound diversity in Hurston's writings, and evidence that perhaps she is even more adept at balancing both of her audiences on the same side of her authorial position—either hypostatically, as with "The Literature of Vivification," or pragmatically, as in "The Literature of Mythification." In her most famous work, *Their Eyes Were Watching God* (1937), her fictional characters resonate with an honesty, and in this case a verisimilitude, for both black and white readers (though perhaps in different ways), while in her autobiography, *Dust Tracks on a Road* (1942), real life blurs with fantasy (again, in different but very real ways to both audiences) to the point that what emerges seems like nothing less than ethnographic myth. The former, of course, represents precisely what the Literature of Vivification will do for a reader; the latter what the Literature of Mythification, at its best, will accomplish.

For example, in *Their Eyes Were Watching God*, Hurston intermingles a variety of narrative dictions:

> Ships at a distance have every man's wish on board. For some they come in with the tide. For others they sail forever on the horizon, never out of sight, never landing until the Watcher turns his eyes away in resignation, his dreams mocked to death by Time. That is the life of men. (1)

> "Naw, Jody, it jus' looks lak it keeps us in some way we ain't natural wid one 'nother. You'se always off talkin' and fixin' things, and Ah feels lak Ah'm jus' markin' time. Hope it soon gets over." (43)

> Then she saw all of the colored people standing up in the back of the courtroom. Packed tight like a case of celery, only much darker than that. They were all against her, she could see. (176)

> "We are handling this case. Another word out of *you*, out of any of you niggers back there, and I'll bind you over to the big court." (178)

The effect of such a polyphony of voices is to create something of a symphony of relationships with her dual audiences. She draws near to one, distances herself from the other, back and forth, playing at times on stereotypes, at other times on deep human emotions that unify readers of all races, yet even at other times portraying situations that equalize readers and characters in sympathetic feeling while using language that would subtly remind readers of a continuing social inequality. The result is to subordinate the ideas conveyed in these passages to the voices that impart them, creating the sense, as does all literature of vivification, that the ideas emerge from the characters and exist for their use, not the author's. Ultimately then, for all readers, it is the characters that live, are vivified, not the author's ideas, and certainly not the author's words. As Cynthia Bond reminds a reader, "The various voices and dictions which constitute the novel's progress are subsumed as a rendering of Janie's life,…a textual recuperation of speakerly rhetoric rather than a valorization of the speakerly as a sufficient, figurally self-reflexive linguistic presence" (215).

By contrast, *Dust Tracks on a Road* offers a fascinating juxtaposition of autobiography, nonchronological and devoid of dates; Hoodoo and "two-headed" witch doctors; initiation rites; songs; and various other anthropological curiosities. It is a narrative which, in spite of its autobiographical rendering, and regardless of any reader's stereotypes or racial folklore, cannot be read strictly literally, or even mildly so, but ascends instead to the level for which it was intended, the level of "autoethnography," the process of defining one's subjective ethnicity as mediated through language, history and ethnographical analysis. In other words, it was intended to foster a level of racial mythology.

As in *Their Eyes Were Watching God*, she foregrounds language, exercising a certain fluidity between the sophisticate and the rube. However, instead of conveying the naturalism of the "real world," code-shifting becomes a vehicle for cultural analysis. At one point, for example, she writes:

> I was a Southerner, and had the map of Dixie on my tongue.…It is an everyday affair to hear somebody called a mullet-headed, mule-eared, wall-eyed, hog-nosed, 'gator-faced, shad-mouthed, screw-necked, goat-bellied, puzzed-gutted, camel-backed, battle-hammed, knock-kneed, razor-legged, box-ankled, shovel-footed, unmated so-and-so!…Since that stratum of the Southern population is not given to book reading, they take their comparisons right out of the barnyard and the woods. When they get through with you, you and your whole family look like an acre of totem-poles. (135–36)

Any critic should immediately identify the myth-making inherent in such narrative. What begins as hyperbole moves seamlessly into cultural analysis, then toward cultural myth, explaining, as myths are designed to do, the idiosyncrasies by which a culture defines itself and interprets its members' behaviors to the broader world.

What should be clear by this point is that such a dialogical approach to African American literature as this is not intended either to expound on prevailing African American literary theory or examine the theoretical influence of Bakhtinian or Buberian philosophy on African American critical thought. It uses both, but is not, in itself, either. This concept is not incompatible with either modern mainstream American realism or with the ideas about black creativity prevalent during the Harlem Renaissance. Both explore literary expression as the function of an individual temperament mediated by the context of a specific environment, and both see the aesthetic value in artistic engagement with societal concerns. Likewise, it is influenced by insights from the very similar dialogical writings of Bakhtin and Buber, but it builds upon those works, not merely encapsulates them. In fact, not to build upon Bakhtin's thought or Buber's, to use the ideas intact, would seem to miss the point of dialogical thought. As the Russian literary critic Sergei Averinstev puts it, "(Bakhtin's) works are not a stockpile of ready-made results which can be mechanically 'applied.' They are something different and larger. They are a source of intellectual energy" (124). The pursuit of that intellectual energy is the goal of this model.

Chapter 2

The Literature of Inversion

One of the nicest things that we created as a generation was just the fact that we could say, "Hey, I don't like white people."

—Nikki Giovanni,
A Dialogue

The Literature of Inversion comprises the most confrontational of African American literary types. From a compositional perspective, an author chooses independence from mainstream literary expectation as the foundation for the creative work in which he or she is engaged, and as a result, prioritizes, subtly or intentionally, the political message of social and literary inversion—black over white. The author's dual audience, of course, perceives the resulting "dialogue" in radically different ways—black audiences, hypostatically; white audiences, pragmatically. As a result, the Literature of Inversion serves to test the boundaries, or literary rules, by which African American literature (as an emerging tradition) might operate before alienating or angering the literary establishment it seeks to join. (At its most extreme, literary works of inversion seek *not* to join the literary establishment, but to spurn it, but this is why Cornel West derogates this kind of literature.)

Using, at its archetypical level, confrontational language and what might be perceived as a caustic disregard for its white audience, the Literature of Inversion often unambiguously portrays white culture as narrow-minded, even simple-minded, violent and merciless, falling far

short morally, if not intellectually, of a sensitive, shrewd, and perspicacious
black America. Seemingly playing on white America's fear of black
America, works of inversion stake out the high ground in what a white
audience would generally perceive to be an adversarial portrayal of racial
issues in America. One significant effect of the Literature of Inversion,
then, is to make the white reader a stranger in his or her own house—the
domicile of language, political power, social hegemony—while conveying
to African American readers an exclusive solidarity of heritage, purpose,
insight, and will.

Henry Dumas's short story "Will the Circle Be Unbroken," from the
collection *Ark of Bones* (1970), offers both an example of the Literature of
Inversion and a metaphor for it. The story details the attempt of a trio of
white sophisticates to infringe upon this African American racial solidarity
by "crashing" a black nightclub, the Sound Barrier Club, to hear one of the
"special times" that a new horn is being played by a black musician named
Probe. The club is closed to white patrons, as one of the trio's previous
attempts to gain entry had demonstrated. Nevertheless, the leader of the
trio, a self-styled "brother" named Jan, had once played with Probe and had
brought his own horn with him this evening, fashioning himself one of the
insiders in the jazz scene. The other two had close connections to the jazz
world, one of them having presumably helped Probe's career with his
published reviews of Probe's music. Despite their "connections," they are
denied permission to enter by the doorman because, he tells them, their race
would make it dangerous for them to hear the music. They understand the
"reason" for the objection, having heard of the "lethal vibrations" created
by the "new sound" of the afro-horn, but they have no historical context
from which to understand its significance, and so they dismiss it as
superstition.

As the black audience, "unaware...of its collectiveness," sways inside
to the music, the trio forces its way into the club with the assistance of a
white policeman sympathetic to their "rights," even though he is
unimpressed by the music itself. "Three ghosts," the narrator calls the gate
crashers, "like chaff blown from a wasteland," and just how superficial they
are soon becomes clear. Before long, Probe begins to play his "afro-horn,"
one of only three in the entire world, and the circle of black identity
tightens, strange vibrations move across the room, and one by one the white

patrons die. As Jan, the last to fall, dies on the floor, remembering how much he dislikes white people, his saxophone case falls open to reveal his shiny instrument, vibrating by itself in what Dumas calls "the freedom of freedom."

The significant detail for understanding the story is that the whites count themselves insiders because they share a common language with those in the club—jazz music. In other words, because they understand the "meaning" of the text, they presume also to know its "theme." However, the "theme," the contextual historic incidence of a specific utterance, is not theirs to know, nor Probe's to provide, but, in Bakhtinian fashion, they begin to discern its dialogical meaning only across the barrier of their intractable otherness, and by then, it is too late (Singer 174). Because the text of the club, Probe's music (clearly portrayed in the story as an Africanism), was so central to the experience within the club, the question being asked by the trio's actions goes to the very essence of Bakhtin's dialogic: Is the utterance from Probe's horn typological, functioning as a trope wherein the word bears a symbolic relationship to its object, signifier to referent, capable of being uttered by a single voice; or is it double-voiced, requiring two distinct voices in dialogue, denoting unfinalizability and pointing to the uniqueness of the resulting image (Bakhtin, *Dialogic Imagination* 327–30, discussed in Morson and Emerson [1990] 324–25). The trio obviously thought it the former; it was, in fact, clearly the latter, leading them to overlook what was a semiotic structure and not merely a model of communication, so that what they presumed to be merely the negotiation of a shared text was instead a "fierce social struggle" (Herrmann 14).

This fierce social struggle is at the epicenter of the Literature of Inversion, perhaps the most distinctive African American literary type which, at its most consequential level, focuses on themes and subject matter which portray black superiority. Toni Cade Bambara is reported to have said that the task of the writer is to make revolution irresistible (J. Bell 30). The Literature of Inversion is black literature's most prominent call to arms. Often dealing with confrontational themes and using provocative titles and language, it confronts its dual audience in a manner that, given its author's race, comes to be viewed by white readers as ideology. White characters in inversive novels and stories are often portrayed as "types"—cruel, simple-minded, transparently racist—and unlike similar portrayals in works of mythification, these white characters never become for white readers antagonistic, and therefore indispensable, components of an emerging and engaging African American myth. Instead, identical to the musical text from Probe's afro-horn, the text of a novel of inversion strikes white readers dead (metaphorically, of course) and serves for black readers as the "closing of the circle." Even among the literary scene's "hippest ofays," those white critics and writers who would, like Jan, Ron, and Tasha, fashion themselves insiders within the African American literati, once inside the "club," all they can bring to it is "alien silence." This is why the Literature of Inversion so successfully satisfies the need in an emerging literary tradition for a literature which tests the boundaries of a mainstream audience's tolerance for the new tradition's idiosyncracies.

African American authors have used a variety of devices to effect its inversion. One particularly transparent device, common among writers of the New Black Aesthetic of the 1960s and revived by self-styled "gangsta rappers" of the 1990s, is the use of angry, often profanity-laced invectives against white America. Amiri Baraka, who changed both his name (from LeRoi Jones) and his literary style in the late 1960s, became especially prominent for his use of such stylistic inversion, penning poetic passages which describe an angry, metaphorically physical relationship with white America, peering out from a hate-filled, foul-smelling white body at "wretched" white women ("An Agony. As Now."), asking that the "bitter bullshit white parts" be left to rot after the body dies and the "sweet meat" of his black consciousness passed along to black America ("leroy"). The anger in his prose is just as clear.

> …the murderous philosophies of the Western white man take many curious forms. And one of the most bizarre methods the man has yet to utilize against black people is to instruct large masses of black people to control their tempers, turn the other cheek, etc., in the presence of, but even more so under the feet and will of, the most brutal killers the world has yet produced. ("The Last Days of the American Empire")

An obvious risk of such a technique, in spite of its effectiveness at social inversion, is that it frequently pushes the boundary of mainstream acceptance too far, and becomes, as Cornel West cautions, an intellectually limiting attempt at creativity which is soon lost amid the artistic isolation that results from it. A more complex, and perhaps more effective, inversive device among African American authors in the last thirty years or so has been a renascent identification of the black writer with Africa. First used with great effect by writers of the Harlem Renaissance in the 1920s, this device offers the African American writer considerably more creative latitude than do angry diatribes, not only for the obvious social reasons, but for its use of more intricate literary tools—tropes and chronotopes rather than just offensive language and ideas. Just as with the rebirth in the 1990s of shocking and profane language among "gangsta rappers," the potential for this re-Africanizing of black artistry to disparage white hegemony did not go unnoticed by the purveyors of popular culture, who profiteered it and, in the process, squandered its influence into that of any other T-shirt slogan.

Its chief literary impact, however, may have been its importance for validating black self-esteem, becoming what critic Clyde Taylor calls "a celebratory, carefree wit…, the alacrity of family reunion, the intoxicating light of new day" (793). Occasionally, the African continent is utilized as the actual setting for a novel or story, as with Alex Haley's *Roots* (1976) or Reginald McKnight's bleak portrait of disease-ridden contemporary Africa in *I Get on the Bus* (1990). However, the myth that accompanies the writer's identification with Africa has nothing to do with geography and everything to do with solidarity. As the captain of Dumas's "Ark of Bones" tells the young caretaker Headeye, "Every African who lives in America has a part of his soul in this ark" (15). In most cases, as Clyde Taylor writes, "the repossession [of "Africa"] has…been lyrical, metaphorical, hallucinatory, mythical, as one grasps the personality of a parent one meets for the first time as an adult" (793). The examples he cites are familiar: the "flying African" motif in Toni Morrison's *Song of Solomon* (1977), Richard Perry's *Montgomery's Children* (1984), and Paule Marshall's *Praisesong for the Widow* (1983); or the contemporary slave ship motif—present-day Africans in the hold of modern cruise ships, as in William Melvin Kelley's *Dunsfords Travels Everywheres* (1970) or boarding an ark with a crew of skeletons to become caretaker of the long-forgotten bones of lynching and Middle Passage victims, as in the title story from Dumas's *Ark of Bones* (793–94). In each case, what emerges from the portrayal is a powerful image that is so effective in romanticizing an

African heritage as to prompt the question of whether this symbol of
"Africa" can ever again be anything so plebeian as a literary figure of
speech, a trope. Bakhtin's writings offer important insight into the question,
and several of his antipodal concepts—trope versus chronotope, theme
versus meaning, monologia versus polyphony—offer a rather clear
distinction between the hypostatic reading (chronotopic, thematic [or
contextual], polyphonic) a black audience would give these works, and the
pragmatic engagement (tropic, explicative, ideological) its white audience
would experience.

The stakes are high. The Bakhtinian perspective on the dialogic
challenges an objectification of the subject by an author, offering instead
a theory of coequal subject positions which are occupied in the course of
negotiating the meaning of the text. This has seldom been the fate of
minority discourse; James A. Miller writes that Bigger Thomas, Richard
Wright's protagonist in *Native Son*, behaves in his self-destructive ways
precisely because he is so overwhelmed by what Bakhtin calls
"authoritative discourse" from the white world, he is forced to externalize
his emotions in order to keep the world at bay (503). That a literature would
self-consciously attempt to "invert" that dynamic exposes precisely the sort
of boundary this type of literature is designed to test. In fact, this resistance
to such authority-bearing speech would constitute exactly the type of
dialogue Bakhtin would most passionately affirm (Steele, *Critical
Confrontations* 32–34). Furthermore, inasmuch as language is an arena of
conflict and confrontation, the white reader stays along for the ride. As a
result, the presence of the Africanist persona in a text, even, as Toni
Morrison points out, in the hands of a white author, has the effect for black
audiences of complicating the text, enriching it and allowing the author to
articulate and portray themes forbidden by the traditional white audience,
much like the blackface minstrel shows allowed an actor to address topics
unapproachable by the white actor behind the make-up (Morrison, *Playing*
66). Much of it, Morrison writes in *Playing in the Dark*, lies in the
subtleties of an author's language:

> A writer's response to American Africanism often provides a subtext that either
> sabotages the surface text's expressed intentions or escapes them through a
> language that mystifies what it cannot bring itself to articulate but still attempts to
> register. [*Author's note: what Morrison describes here, it seems, is (a) the*

Literature of Subversion and (b) the Literature of Inversion.] Linguistic responses to Africanism serve the text by further problematizing its matter with resonances and luminations. They can serve as allegorical fodder for the contemplation of Eden, expulsion, and the availability of grace. They provide paradox, ambiguity; they strategize omissions, repetitions, disruptions, polarities, reifications, violence. In other words, they give the text a deeper, richer, more complex life than the sanitized one commonly presented to us. (66)

The focus of Morrison's essay is actually the use of the African figure in white canonical literature, but as diverse as the utilization of Africanism is in American literature, Morrison's concerns address issues that affect the black writer as much as the white writer:

- the Africanist character as surrogate and enabler, or in other words, the manner in which the Africanist image allows authors to conceptualize complex or abstract issues,
- the use of the Africanist idiom to designate categories of space and time, like a Bakhtinian chronotope, drawing racial distinctions of class or cognitive differences,
- the use of Africanist character to contrast and define whiteness as a category, and
- the use of Africanist narrative to allow self-reflection on social history and circumstance. (51–53)

To raise the question, as Morrison does, of a white author's right to utilize this "myth of Africa" only validates its importance for the Literature of Inversion, a literature which seeks, by definition, to exclude the white voice. What is striking about Morrison's analyses, in the context of this theory, is that, even though her conclusions address the utilization of Africanism by white authors, her challenge against the appropriation of the image by the white "authoritative voice" would preclude not only its use by a white author, but its dialogical use between black author and white audience. This is precisely the circumstance which creates the Literature of Inversion; white audiences have no choice but to view the resulting text as monologistic and authoritarian. The problem with the authoritative word, Bakhtin writes, is that it demands, because its authority has already been affirmed in a past considered to be "hierarchically higher" than the present, that we do nothing more than simply acknowledge its authority. It is "indissolubly fused with its authority—with political power, an institution, a person—and it stands and falls together with that authority" (*Dialogic Imagination* 342–43).

What Morrison suggests, then, is that the Literature of Inversion is an appropriate black response to a social context and literary heritage that has been, in the past, authoritatively defined by those outside it. In truth, the recapturing of the Africanist image, and of the voice to define it, has deep roots in Pan-African and African American ideas about language and its social role. Kofi Anyidoho notes that "The historical and contemporary dilemma in which African peoples find themselves reflects a crisis of consciousness, or rather a crisis of lack of consciousness....To deal with this crisis of consciousness, we must first of all turn our full attention to 'that most manifest and coherent of all cultural systems—language'" (46).

The question, then, for both Pan-African and African American writers is whether the language of colonialism can be salvaged and transformed to meet the creative needs of the colonialized. For African American writers, the question is a complex and subtle one, both linguistically and thematically, but is clearly the same question as the one addressed by African writers over the English language itself, and whether it must be accepted, or transformed, or finally abandoned completely for some "mother tongue" or newer native language (Anyidoho 47). The question is far from rhetorical; in Africa, the word (*nommo*) creates reality, and whoever possesses the word, possesses reality (Byerman 6). Chinua Achebe insists that colonial languages were tacitly, but reluctantly, accepted by Africans, and the result, for many, is a "first" language that is, in fact, a foreign language. Marlene Nourbese Philip drives that point deeply into the heart of the matter in her poem "Discourse on the Logic of Language," from her award-winning *She Tries Her Tongue: Her Silence Softly Breaks*. Throughout the poem, she uses the metaphor of a "mother tongue" to suggest that she has neither a mother nor a tongue, a language, but nevertheless dazzles the reader with how masterfully she co-opts the English language to convey the alienation she feels in using it, such as when she transforms the words "English" and "language" into "anguish" and then shatters her readers' expectations with the phrase "English is a foreign *anguish*" (emphasis added).

Clearly, the issue of a "colonial language" is much more complex when applied to writers of the diaspora. Critic Henry Louis Gates, in *The Signifying Monkey* (1988), suggests that Afro-American writers experience unique demands to confront and resolve the Bakhtinian concept of "double-voiced discourse," particularly the hidden polemic. "Double-voicing," Bakhtin posits, refers to the utterance that embodies both the speaker's point of view and the second speaker's simultaneous evaluation of that utterance, decolonized for black purposes, Gates writes, "by inserting a new semantic orientation into a word which already has—and retains—its own orientation" (Gates 50). Some critics consider Gates vague, and perhaps even misleading, in his application of Bakhtin's ideas to African American literature (Steele, "Metatheory" 480–482), but at its most consequential level, particularly for this model, the utility Gates provides for Bakhtin's double-voicing is in a self-referential intertextuality, which he calls "Signifyin(g)," and the role it plays for African American authors in differentiating a black narrative style. From that perspective, a double-voicing of the myth of Africa from its white "authoritative discourse," as discussed by Morrison, to the African American intraracial "dialogue" of this theory might also be considered an example.

The resulting race-based distinction between polyphonic and monologic discursive images of Africa might potentially be framed in Saussurean terms of *langue* and *parole*, but Bakhtin rejected that purely linguistic distinction for a more productive focus on the role of social evaluation in concrete utterances. The attempt to explore the "value judgment" inherent in a dialogical utterance led Bakhtin to examine the dialectical relationship between two key aspects of the utterance—its "theme," which refers to the unrepeatable and contextual historic incidence of an utterance, and its "meaning," the pseudo-fixed, concrete, and repeatable self-identical component of an utterance. "Meaning" may be said to be fixed by use, but within the contradiction between that fixity and the interpretive element of it resides the semantico-ideological aspect that is unique within it and indissolubly connected to the context of its use, which would convey its "theme" (Ponzio 399). V. N. Volosinov, one of the Bakhtin circle often thought to be Bakhtin himself, writes that "a change in meaning is essentially always a reevaluation: the transposition of some particular word from one evaluative context to another" (*Marxism and the Philosophy of Language*, quoted in Singer 179). In that case, the only way for an African American author to transform the "meaning" of the myth of Africa for a white reader would be to transform its "theme," which would, according to Bakhtin, transform not only the relationship between theme and meaning, but between the "self" and "other" inherent in the dialogical negotiation of the Africanist image. For the Literature of Inversion, however, keeping the white reader focused on meaning, ideology, is precisely the point.

The authorial technique of appropriating the text from its white readers can be demonstrated by, and is at the same time the subject of, the Henry Dumas short story "Fon," another work from the collection *Ark of Bones*. The story is like an archetypical black fantasy—a lynching in which the victim turns the table on his white executioners and, through supernatural intervention, kills them all. As with many of Dumas's stories, the literary structure is not particularly complex, and the symbolism either flagrantly obvious or baffling in its obscurity, yet this story, like his others, engages the reader "in a shifting, ritualistic dance along the ghostly corridor separating Africa and America" (Gilbert 240). The story hammers incessantly at the distinction between the "meaning"-bound rednecks, who understand well the fixed (for them) meaning of an act of vandalism and a nearby slow-witted black boy, the mysterious Fon, whose contextual explanations of the events are so unbelievable that the whites appear not even to hear them at all. The episode begins when an angry white redneck named Nillmon ("nothing man") has his rear windshield broken by a flaming rock and stops the car to find the vandal. He searches the nearby community of Canebrake, a shanty village abandoned years before by its black residents and now, according to an old redneck friend of Nillmon's, haunted, and though he sees an old woman rocking on a porch and what appears to be a worship service in progress at a nearby church, he leaves empty-handed. Returning to his car, he discovers a "half-wit nigger" boy sitting on the billboard from which the rock apparently came, "with his brother" the boy says, although Nillmon sees no one else anywhere in the vicinity.

The apparent difference in what Nillmon and Fon *see* is at the heart of all that follows. Nillmon asks Fon why he threw the rock; Fon replies that no one *threw* the rock. Nillmon presumes Fon to be helping his brother vandalize the cars of passing white motorists; Fon says he is teaching his brother to "shoot arrows." Nillmon imagines emptying his pistol into Fon's head, and does everything he can to frighten Fon, but it is obvious to Nillmon that "This Fon nigger ain't scared." The frustration of this dialogue, along with having to wait for an endless progression of cattle being herded by a black boy and his dog across the road in front of them, distracts Nillmon enough to allow Fon to get out of the back seat of the car and simply walk away. It is, in one sense, a humorous event, reminiscent of the episode in *Uncle Tom's Cabin* when the slaves Sam and Andy confuse and manipulate the slavecatcher Haley with all manner of doubletalk. In fact, the effect is the same, creating a social inversion by mocking an arrogant bigwig to his face without his realizing it. Dumas inverts, as well, the lynching which seems about to occur by focusing repeatedly on, not Fon's neck, but Nillmon's. Early in the story, Nillmon "snaps his neck" for a second look at the road. Shortly after they meet, Fon, instead of looking into Nillmon's eyes, "rivets his eyes on the white man's neck." Later, then, as the lynching is played out, its literal inversion comes as no surprise.

After Fon's escape, Nillmon rounds up his buddies and returns to Canebrake, in spite of the old man's warning, and finds the "church service" still in progress and Fon waiting in the doorway of the cabin where the woman was rocking on the porch. They shove Fon into the car again, and are again stopped, not by cattle this time, but by a column of black people in the road. "Those are my brothers," Fon tells the men. The rednecks race on through the crowd, which shouts in some supernatural sound when they see Fon inside the car. Soon the men stop, pull Fon out, and proceed with their attempts at lynching him, in spite of their frustration at not having yet frightened him. Suddenly, however, first one of them, then another, finally Nillmon himself, is shot through the neck by an arrow from the darkness. "That was mighty close," Fon thinks, "but it is better this way. To have looked at them would have been too much. Four centuries of black eyes burning into four weak white men...would've set the whole earth on fire. Not yet, not yet" (111). He returns to the church with "one more black stone" for the tower they are building there.

It is a classic inversion, not only seizing control of what white America presumes to be a *shared* text, as in "Will the Circle Be Unbroken?" but seizing control of the social text white America still presumes to be in its own authoritative voice. It is a masterful use of Bakhtin's "carnival"; by destroying the white reader's old images and old uses for words, works of inversion present "a new sense of all old words, things and concepts...by freeing them temporarily of all semantic links, and freely recreating them" (*Rabelais* 463). Such use of carnival may, in fact, always be a part of the "fierce social struggle" of race.

This is the essence of the mythification of "Africa," and why such self-referential efforts serve to embrace the black reader and distance themselves from the white reader. To the degree that a concept such as "Africa" *must* have its "meaning"—as a metaphor for some essentialism in blackness, as a representation of diaspora, as (to quote popular culture's too extreme appropriation of it) some "black thing" that outsiders "wouldn't understand"—it becomes for the white reader a trope: single-voiced, authoritative discourse. The security in that position for African American literature is that it provides the black reader continuity and closure, but at the price of becoming a "crisis" text, a text that seeks to silence the challenge of theoretical criticism through the appeal to a privileged voice (Natoli 15).

The danger accompanying that claim is that, while it may satisfy for a time the demands placed upon the tradition for unity or essentiality, it ultimately does risk becoming uniquely a "black thing," the African American literary tradition's own "madwoman in the attic." Cornell West referred to this type of African American literature as "Going It Alone," high on emotional energy but intellectually limited, focused as it is on narrow African American themes. Henry Louis Gates notes that the African American tradition may be read as "successive attempts to create new narrative space for representing the recurring referent of Afro-American literature, the so-called Black Experience" (*Signifying Monkey* 111). By "referent," he seems to refer not to Bakhtin's "meaning," the repeatable, self-identical component of an utterance, but "theme," the contextual historic incidence of utterance, secured through heteroglossia, double-voicing, one speech act undergirding the foundation of another and in turn being influenced prior to its utterance by that second, yet unuttered speech. That the Literature of Inversion could be seen that way by black readers, while white readers see it as an unsuccessful attempt at monological mythification, only accentuates the double consciousness with which a black writer is forced to work.

Furthermore, the tradition is written in English, a language at odds with the myth of "Africa," denying it and negating it in its tropological uses, but manifesting in the process precisely the essence of double-voicing, in which the utterance—"Africa" in English—becomes the inevitable result of both black and white influences. The effect, then, is to place such self-referential themes as the myth of "Africa" not in the position of Dumas's Probe, wreaking destruction through its authoritative message, but in the position of his white trio in the jazz club, whose very survival depends upon their ability to participate in the dialogic, negotiating meaning rather than holding on to a previous one. However, they are unable to do that, as white readers are unable to do with works of inversion. It is in that sense, for both black and white readers, that the Literature of Inversion is so carnivalesque.

It is also an essential purview of African American literature (as opposed to African American music, culture, or even popular culture). If the novel, and by extension the short story, mediates a reader's understanding of the world through negotiated meaning, through dialogic, rather than through tropes of identity, then Bakhtin is correct in asserting its supremacy in expressing the struggle of historical existence in the human subject (Singer 174). As a result, the myth of "Africa" should be understood by black readers, subconsciously in most cases, as something similar to a Bakhtinian "chronotope," a powerful literary way of understanding experience that, consistent with the Einsteinian concept of "time-space" (its literal meaning), acknowledges the "wholeness," the intrinsic interconnection, of space and time (Morson and Emerson 366–69). Because of its specular nature, it reveals the context behind what the reader is reading, covering the blind spots of a genre, negotiating the fields of historical, biographic, and social relations of literature and life, not so much the focus of our attention, but the ground for that upon which our attention is focused. This is precisely what a hypostatic relationship between author and audience would entail, and as a result, it is the bridge for black readers between the real and represented worlds of African American experience.

Jean Toomer's *Cane* demonstrates well this application of the chronotope to the myth of "Africa," so deeply integrated is the myth within the tone and events of the novel. *Cane* engages the myth through the back door—positing a dark counter-myth of "America," the America that the "flying Africans" are always leaving. Part I might be called "the macabre carnival," because Toomer transforms warm, nostalgic images—

motherhood, childhood, religion, community, sunset—into frightening new images with "new and unexpected juxtapositions." His "Portrait in Georgia," for example, sees a woman's braided hair as lyncher's rope, her lips as scars and blisters, and her slim white flesh as the ashes left behind after a lynching. It is a portrait of "America" that black readers find familiar, and would have, even more so, in 1922 when the book was published. A product of his time and heritage, Toomer's Ralph Kabnis, from Part III of *Cane*, verbalizes the hypostasis of the myth in describing his own identity: "Th whole world is a conspiracy t sin, especially in America," he shouts, "an against me. I'm the victim of their sin" (236). Toomer's America, especially the rural South portrayed in Part I and to which Kabnis returns in Part III, is emotional and immediate, yet at the same time comprises such a conspiracy of ignorance that it seems inescapably cold and passionless—a beautiful child frolicking in the sunset before having, and killing, an illegitimate baby; near-white beauty lusting for the fantasy of negritude and desire; a violence that flows naturally out of southern eroticism, anger, and sexual values (male, female, black, white) under a strange "red nigger moon...blood-burning moon." Toomer's characters seem bound to an emotional roller-coaster, still enslaved to this particular place and culture. Even childhood offers no sanctuary; Esther, at nine, is but a prologue to the time when she, as an adult (and a poor example of one), can play out her role in the oppressive racial and sexual politics of the time. This is a society in which life is made to appear ordained and orderly, yet Toomer makes it feel dirty and oppressively claustrophobic.

This is the "America" of Ralph Kabnis's search for identity, which he defines in terms evocative of a Bakhtinian dialogic:

> Those words I was tellin y about, they wont fit int th mold thats branded on m soul....Th form thats burned int my soul is some twisted awful thing that crept in from a dream, a godam nightmare, an wont stay still unless I feed it. An it lives on words. Not beautiful words. God Almighty no. Misshapen, split-gut, tortured, twisted words. Layman was feedin it back there that day you thought I ran out fearin things. Niggers, black niggers feed it cause theyre evil an their looks are words. Yallar niggers feed it. This whole damn bloated purple country feeds it cause its goin down t hell in a holy avalanche of words. (224)

Kabnis feels himself incapable of dialogue regarding his own creative oration because anything that might invite such a dialogue is undercut by the authoritative discourse inherent in those southern surroundings. Though Kabnis may have migrated back to the South with the intention of dialogue with the social text of the Negro's position in that society, he clearly does not now believe that to be a possibility, and so he finds himself being left with only one alternative—to turn upon himself and his race and the anger of being subordinated to the monologic judgment of whites and their compliant Negro lackies. He views the old slave Father John as a chief symbol of that, calling him the "Father of Satan" and "old black bastard" and confronting him with his doubts and anger in the cellar below Halsey's workshop—"he ain't my past," Kabnis says of Father John. "My ancestors were Southern blue-bloods."

This rejection of the authoritative white social text is precisely where the Literature of Inversion finds its signature in contemporary African American literature, and not coincidently, often the point at which the myth of "Africa" is most clearly differentiated in the interpretations given it by its dual audience. What is for white readers simply a metaphor expands for black readers into something deeper, something quasi-chronotopic. Bakhtin explains that, in the chronotope, "spatial and temporal marks are fused into a meaningful and concrete whole. Time here thickens, grows denser, becomes artistically visible; likewise, space becomes more intense and drawn into the movement of time, plot, history…, artistically assimilating time and space in the novel, and thus for assuring its unity" (*Dialogic Imagination* 84–86). Precisely like "the rogue, the clown, and the fool [who] create around themselves their particular little worlds, their particular chronotopes" (*Dialogic Imagination* 159), the figure of the American Negro is that of the outsider who exists in a chronotope of his or her own. As a result, the "chronotope" of "Africa" may bear much in common with Bakhtin's chronotope of threshold. The threshold, as used extensively by Dostoevsky, refers to that point in a character's life denoted by crisis or "break," when decisions are boldly made or fear (of crossing the threshold) melts into indecision (*Dialogic Imagination* 248). Malcolm V. Jones writes that it is "typified by the knife-edge of deconstruction, of the confrontation and reversal of oppositions, of resurrections, renewals, epiphanies, the uncanny, ecstasy and the abyss…" (117). This sounds like a description of "Fon" or "Will the Circle Be Unbroken?" or even the more realistic "Kabnis"; time and space fall out of biographical time and seem to merge, so that the myth of "Africa" incorporates nothing of the contemporary geographical entity, but represents instead a timeless place that may easily be wherever, or whenever, the protagonist is, as with the boat full of African spirits collecting the bones of the victims of American racism in "Ark of Bones."

In that sense, Ralph Kabnis's obsession with religion has nothing to do with theology or its emotional sentiment, but with the precision with which it differentiates the options from the social threshold at which he stands. This was the issue for many blacks. Those who moved north in search of a new life often found themselves radically disrupted from the familiar and comforting authority of their southern faith systems and its spiritual hegemony. In a very real way, this is the chronotope for this story, the "Africa" for black Americans of the 1920s. For Kabnis, religion brings a compression of time and space, representing the South he once knew before moving north and the South to which he had returned, embodied now in the character of Samuel Hanby, the principal at Kabnis's school. Hanby represents a compliant lackey to white America, a reminder of the Booker T. Washington who had become so repulsive to Negro intellectuals of the time. Toomer describes him as "a well-dressed, smooth, rich, black-skinned Negro who thinks there is no one quite so suave and polished as himself....he affects the manners of a wealthy white planter" (185). He fires Kabnis for damaging the image of the race with his drunkenness, which only confirms for Kabnis, as he stands at yet another threshold, the power of the white "authoritative discourse" to which he feels subjected. He wants to avenge his firing with violence, "else the power of direction will completely slip from him to those outside" (189). He does not, however, being interrupted by Lewis, a figure who, like Kabnis, is from the North, and whose militant authority, like an alternative authoritative discourse, resembles that of W.E.B. Du Bois.

Kabnis, in effect, moves through the entire story on the threshold of monological disengagement. In a world of Bakhtinian heteroglossia, all attempts at monological discourse can, and should be, challenged, yet Kabnis cannot separate himself from his past experiences, and so is willing to grant spurious authoritative meanings to social texts even in the face of contrasting evidence. The result, Malcolm Jones writes, is "violent oscillation," instability, a threshold in which the character faces "a world and individuals poised on the knife-edge of viability and non-viability, almost real but not quite" (30). So Kabnis moves from threshold to threshold, progressing almost literally through the psychological thresholds identified by Bakhtin in Dostoevsky's work: the threshold between wakefulness and sleep (Kabnis struggles to find sleep, and calls himself "a dream"), reality and fantasy (imagining himself being chased by "slavehunters"), sanity and madness, self-consciousness and the abyss (finding his self-identity in a cellar) (Jones 56). Subjected as he is to racist self-identity, Kabnis draws an erroneous distinction between himself and his world, and prays that God will allow him to preserve that distinction by making the world ugly, saving him from the torture of its beauty. He presumes a message thrown through the window at Fred Halsey's house—"You northern nigger, its time fer y t leave. Git along now"—to be written by whites and intended for him, and he races from the house, overcome by fear and wild scenarios of slavehunters and dogs on his trail, in spite of the casual manner with which his hosts regard the note (179–83). He is, in Bakhtinian terms, "on the road," and once there, Bakhtin says:

the spatial and temporal paths of the most varied people—representatives of all social classes, estates, religions, nationalities, ages—intersect at one spatial and temporal point. People who are normally kept separate by social and spatial distance can accidentally meet; any contrast may crop up, the most various fates may collide and interweave with one another..., even as they become more complex and more concrete by the collapse of *social distances*. (243–44)

It is, like the myth of "Africa" itself, a paradigm of encounter, and at the same time Kabnis is on his actual "roads"—from his room to Fred Halsey's house, back to his room, to Halsey's workshop, to the cellar—he is clearly on a psychological road leading to an encounter with himself. Struggling with sleeplessness, Kabnis finds himself at the beginning of a journey whose origin is established for him by the juxtaposition of two avenues on which he finds himself—he is *returning* to the South after years in the North, and at the same time engaging his self-concept in a dialogue of *progressive* psychological development (Patterson 26). No matter whether the journey is forward or backward, it posits a new beginning at every crossroads, yet another threshold to be crossed. His dialogue with himself is discursive, and would be so even were it not verbalized, and so it leads

Kabnis, even through an imaginary other, back to himself (as would any discourse). "The face comes to life," David Patterson writes, "with utterance born of encounter" (103).

Because the Literature of Inversion is hypostatic only in its "black author/black reader" dialogic, it is Kabnis's encounter with his own black face that Toomer seems at pains to show the reader. "Whoever you are," he has Kabnis say, "do not think that the *face* that rests beside you is the real Kabnis. Ralph Kabnis is a dream. And dreams are *faces* with large eyes and weak chins and broad brows that get smashed by the fists of square *faces*....The dream is a soft *face* that fits uncertainly....If I, the dream...could become the *face* of the South..." (158, emphasis added). In the absence of a convincing Africanist myth, a comforting reassurance that previous (or even contemporary) Negroes had already crossed the threshold and claimed their own identity by flying back to Africa or calling down supernatural avengers, Kabnis, like the black "everyman" who is the protagonist of *Cane*, is left to cross the threshold on his own, by violently reviling his past and himself in an orgy of self-hatred, then rising like the resurrected Jesus in a near-ecstatic trance to engage the present (230–37). It seems to work. Once he rises from the cellar, Kabnis sees a new world: "the sun arises from its cradle in the tree-tops of the forest. Shadows of pines are dreams the sun shades from its eyes. The sun rises. Gold-glowing child, it steps into the sky and sends a birth-song slanting down gray dust streets and sleepy windows of the southern town" (237).

The Literature of Inversion is a literature rooted in black hope, because the works themselves are, by definition, rooted in a conscious portrayal of black superiority. Even when the protagonist's future is ambiguous, as Kabnis's is, or is awash in racial injustice and loss, as in Dumas's "Rope of Wind," the Literature of Inversion looks beyond the realism of social circumstance (even while portraying it) to a transcendent time and space where African American salvation is assured. The tragedy in Dumas's and Toomer's stories is not that someone might die, but that someone might choose not to die when "the chosen" need it and when he or she has been anointed for such a task. This is the myth of "Africa," and why it is so important to the Literature of Inversion. Its legacy is the sense of community that comes when black readers conceptualize the myth as a mediation of their own consciousness and recognize that, were it not for the potential to conceptualize and communicate the inversions from which their racial consciousness is born, they would remain as objectified as the white readers for whom the myth means nothing.

Chapter 3
The Literature of Subversion

Early in Ralph Ellison's *Invisible Man*, the young nameless protagonist confesses to having been cursed by overhearing his grandfather's dying words. His grandfather had been a meek and compliant black "citizen," so much so that those around the old man at his death thought he had gone mad, so completely unexpected were his words:

> Son, after I'm gone I want you to keep up the good fight. I never told you, but our life is a war and I have been a traitor all my born days, a spy in the enemy's country ever since I give up my gun back in the Reconstruction. Live with your head in the lion's mouth. I want you to overcome 'em with yeses, undermine 'em with grins, agree 'em to death and destruction, let 'em swoller you till they vomit or bust wide open. (16)

The subversion he describes has been a surreptitious part of African American culture for four hundred years; that it would become a part of Afro-American literature is certainly reasonable. The literary dynamic would be identical to the social instruction in the old man's dying words—a narrative whose verisimilitude for white audiences is so convincing that black audiences sometimes express anger or incredulity at the author's pragmatic compliance with white expectation, like the college student who casually discounted Shelby Steele's work because, as she put it, "he's not really black."

To the contrary, however, literary works of subversion are often remarkable in the complexity with which the author undercuts social and literary conventions and structures. In an emerging literary tradition, in fact, the Literature of Subversion is unique in its purpose of solidifying a group self-identity through subversive appropriation of accepted forms and devices. Of course, the better an author understands those traditional forms and devices, the more effective the subversion. One reason, then, for the complexity of this form resides in what Mikhail Bakhtin would call the African American author's "creative understanding" of white culture, in which "outsideness is the most powerful lever of understanding (*Speech Genres* 7). In contrast to the Literature of Inversion's centrifugal force, like an explosion of black emotion, works of subversion move inward, centripetally, tightening the interaction between white and black, and undercutting conventions by which racial distinction is maintained. In effect, the narrator is intervening clandestinely, subversively, in the characters' experiences, often without a white reader's knowledge (though almost inevitably with a black reader's). It is, perhaps, the literary equivalent of the "cakewalk," a comic processional from antebellum plantations where slaves were forced to dress up in finery cast off by their masters, and strut pretentiously around the dance floor. While the white slave masters laughed at the slaves' "futile" attempts at refinement, the slaves laughed even harder (and of course later) at the subversive ridicule they were heaping upon their masters. The result, of both the cakewalk and the Literature of Subversion, is the possibility of fulfilling W.E.B. Du Bois's goal (albeit not exactly as he intended) of besting white America at its own game. Moreover, inasmuch as Bakhtin insists that the most competent position from which to address a culture is as an outsider equipped with some—not all, but some—insider skills, the black author may even be writing from a position of superiority. Darryl Pinckney's protagonist in *High Cotton* stakes out such a position from the beginning.

By the time the nameless protagonist in *High Cotton* goes to work for the renowned white author Djuna Barnes at a key juncture midway through the novel, he has already engaged the reader with a long comic history of his eccentric, black middle-class extended family and their relatively successful attempts at seeming less black and more middle-class. Their influence upon the protagonist is crucial in understanding the novel and Barnes's role in it, which ultimately opens the door to some illumination about Pinckney's double-conscious relationship with *High Cotton*'s dual audience. The protagonist and narrator is a fourth-generation college graduate who uses his race in whatever way seems most immediately advantageous, which makes him so enigmatic in his search for an identity that, even given a Hollywood ending in which he apparently experiences a kind of self-revelatory epiphany, he emerges at the end of the novel as mysterious as he is at the beginning.

"No one sat me down and told me I was a Negro," he says in the novel's opening, before proceeding to recount his picaresque adventure through a familiar white world, or at least a heavily bleached black one, where no one seems to have told anyone who is a Negro—growing up in a white suburban elementary school; trips to London, to his grandfather's Congregational church in Louisville, to his Aunt Clara's house in Opelika; his education at Columbia University, followed by an extended stay in New York City, where he worked briefly for Djuna Barnes doing odd jobs; forays into black militancy. Throughout the journey, he alternates between, on the one hand, denying his race and his past, and, on the other, using it to impress his white liberal friends. Richard Eder concludes that "Pinckney is on what may be an impossible search…a search for language to speak of himself in" (3). This is, of course, the precise dilemma of the subversive author, who must, as Ellison's character reminds the reader, "live in the lion's mouth," where "the lion's" language lives as well. The language Pinckney ultimately chooses becomes a key to deciphering the subversion of this novel; the narrative is full of cultural references, often with subtle but sharp-witted connotations, especially among a bourgeois white audience. However, even more significantly, out of the implied juxtaposition of *his* language with Djuna Barnes's literary language emerges a complex series of metaphors rooted in the characters and style of Barnes's most famous work, *Nightwood*. Given the protagonist's ambiguous racial identity, the juxtaposition is not insignificant. Mikhail Bakhtin notes that, "when there is no access to one's own personal 'ultimate' word, then every thought, feeling, experience must be refracted through someone else's style, someone else's manner, with which it cannot immediately be merged without reservation, without distance, without refraction" (*Problems* 202). The refraction of Pinckney's dichotomous (double-conscious) language through Barnes's privileged, but equally dichotomous (male-female, sexually ambiguous), language significantly alters the approach from which his story must be read. With its use of marginalized characters and disquieting sexual themes, Barnes's *Nightwood* provides Pinckney an ideal conduit for cultural subversion. Its characters are not unlike white America's stereotypes of blacks—specimens of outrageous behavior growing from complex psychological and cultural needs. Most notable in this characterization is *Nightwood*'s protagonist, Robin Vote, a mysterious bestial woman whose emotional presence thematically shadows the last half of *High Cotton*, illuminating and directing the path by which its narrator comes to acknowledge his own mysterious identity. That *High Cotton*'s protagonist seems to be seeking his identity in white America and finding it in a dark, idiosyncratic metaphor of decadence would be subversive enough, but the idea that the entire search is a complex literary sleight-of-hand which frustrates the white reader's expectation for black literature enables Pinckney to fabricate the ultimate subversion—undermining the white reader's ability to dictate and control the text.

As in *Nightwood*, the narrator's past is an essential prologue to the story of *High Cotton*. In fact, Pinckney's narrator is born into a family populated by an entire generation of social climbers like *Nightwood*'s Felix Volkbein, a self-conscious Jew who seeks entry into Europe's most exclusive circles by inventing self-important titles and histories for himself. Just as Felix "felt that the great past might mend a little if he bowed low enough, if he succumbed and gave homage" (9), the prideful family in *High Cotton* pursues its own manner of historical revision. Aunt Clara refers to herself as a "high yellow" and refuses to be buried beside her husband because he is interred in a cemetery on the wrong side of town. Uncle Ulysses "never bought black in his life," mistrusting anything that seems to have been intended for black consumption. Grandfather Eustice, the narrator's alter ego, is a Congregationalist minister who presumes himself to be superior to his parishioners, having taken his education at Harvard and Brown, and consistently frustrates them with his high church worship styles. In fact, the narrator himself follows closely in their footsteps, navigating his way with ease through white suburbs and *haute bourgeois* friends, creating what must appear to white readers as a "homage" to white culture. Among his regular soliloquies on the difficulties of being a member of the "Also Chosen," he confesses that "I carried props on the subway—the latest *Semiotext(e)*, a hefty volume of the Frankfurt School—so that the employed would not get the wrong idea or, more to the point, the usual idea about me. I did not want them to take me for another young prole" (193).

Into this mix eventually appears the iconoclastic author Djuna Barnes, who is by the time of her appearance in the book less than a year from her death.[1] Her appearance in the novel is late, two-thirds of the way through the book, and she flickers by so rapidly—fewer than ten pages—that the reader is left echoing the words of one of her own characters, Felix Volkbein: "If I should try to put into words, I mean how I did see her, it would be incomprehensible, for the simple reason that I find that I never did have a really clear idea of her at any time. I had an image of her, but that is not the same thing. An image is a stop the mind makes between uncertainties" (111). Nevertheless, her presence so shapes the novel from that point forward that literary critic Edmund White calls her "the muse" for *High Cotton*. His intent is certainly not to suggest a stylistic inspiration; *High Cotton* is written in a realistic style that departs significantly from the modernist surrealism of *Nightwood*. Perhaps what happens to the book with Barnes's appearance is closer to the Bakhtinian ideal of interconnection without semiotic homology. Certainly one of Barnes's most pointed contributions is to remind a reader familiar with *Nightwood* of the fluidity with which *High Cotton*'s protagonist, like all five of *Nightwood*'s main characters, moves from identity to identity. One of *Nightwood*'s strangest characters, Dr. Matthew O'Connor, the book's figurative "Greek chorus," states the case quite directly: "I'm not able to stay permanent unless you help me, O Book of Concealment!" (132). Permanence is an elusive feature for Pinckney's narrator as well; he not only roams through an emotionally ambiguous racial identity, he has also been through five jobs before the one he takes as Barnes's adjutant—waiter, office temp, auditor, telephone salesman, bookstore clerk—and has been fired from all five, seeming almost oblivious to the social consequences of being black.

Even more subtle, however, is the manner in which the protagonist's journey through a white society is placed into focus by the metaphorical comparison of the protagonist with *Nightwood*'s protagonist, Robin Vote. Pinckney uses language like a secret code at this point. When the protagonist enters Djuna Barnes's apartment for the first time, he notes the diminutive size of the home by calling it "brutally cramped—one tiny, *robin*'s egg" (195, emphasis added). Later, he spots several small phials that he describes as "solemn as *vot*ive candles" (202, emphasis added). In this story of a man who looks black and lives white, and seems uncertain of his identity, the reference to Robin Vote cannot be accidental.

Particularly important is the image of the "robin's egg." Robin's pregnancy in *Nightwood* is not a good one for her—the baby is malformed for this world and is quickly abandoned (48–9). Even during the pregnancy, Robin confesses to being "aware of some lost land" inside her, and so, like the protagonist of *High Cotton*, she begins wandering the countryside, through cities, as far as the trains might take her, eventually "halfway to Berlin" (coincidently, perhaps, where Pinckney himself wound up writing *High Cotton*) (45). The protagonist, a black intellectual in a white society, is clearly in the "Robin's egg," the lost land, and seems quite malfitted to the world into which he has been delivered, as well. The result is a clear metaphorically Oedipal bonding of the protagonist with Robin. Both are dualistic, yet in contrasting, or perhaps harmonious, ways. She is female, but dresses and looks like a boy; he is black, but acts and talks like the white society with which he was reared.

Though the protagonist often gives a reader the sense that what is being said in the novel is intended for his own private consumption, like a student writing in a journal, his story plays word games and offers witty allusions to popular culture in a manner that makes clear his "sideward glance" toward both audiences he knows to be accompanying him on this journey. His first statement reveals his burden: "No one sat me down and told me I was a Negro" (3). For that reason, he is, like Robin, "an infected carrier of the past" (37). Clearly, his past becomes his defining feature; the richly detailed, often warmly humorous tales of his ancestors carry the novel through its earliest stages. As with Robin, the relationship of the protagonist and his past is one of alternating attraction and repulsion. Indeed, the novel finds its ultimate focus in the protagonist's understanding, first at a subconscious level, then finally at the literal level, that he is a present-day reflection of his haughty Grandfather Eustice (Gates, "The Great Black Hope" 9). As a result, the protagonist often refuses to look back, using language that echoes Robin's timelessness even early in the story. "I couldn't allow myself to look back," he says, "having presented myself to myself as one who had never been anywhere but where I was" (86). Although his attempts to come to an understanding of his racial identity drive the book, he clearly seeks the understanding for personal, not social reasons; he has no interest in what "being black" means to others (Fein 17). In that sense, he is a reflection of Robin, the somnambulist, who walks through life as though in a dream, "at once completely egotistical and yet lacking in a sense of her own identity" (Frank 33–34). In the same manner, Robin's description as "outside the 'human type'" (146) serves well as a metaphor for the protagonist's struggle to free himself from society's expectations, or at least to free himself in his own mind to become a singular unified being. He offers some insight into his dilemma late in the story:

> The ledger of how to be simultaneously yourself and everyone else who might observe you, the captain's log of travel in the dual consciousness, the white world as the deceptive sea and the black world as the armed galley, gave me the comic feeling that I was living alongside myself, that there was me and a ventriloquist's replica of me on my lap, and that both of us awaited the intervention of a third me, the disembodied me, before we could begin the charade of dialogue. (220)

This is a remarkably candid description of the black author's situation in approaching his or her dual audience, and clearly the words (and the entire experience) are as much Pinckney's as they are this unnamed protagonist's. For an author as comfortable in white society as Pinckney—someone who has, as Bakhtin would suggest, surrounded himself with as much difference as possible—subversive wordplay, cultural referents, and symbolism become the logical response to the dilemma.

Nevertheless, if the uncertainty of racial identity is the accident that brings together the protagonist and Djuna Barnes, the acknowledgment of its reality becomes the occasion for their separation. Barnes orders the protagonist to wash a blouse in the sink, and when he refuses, she stops herself, too late, from making an unflattering remark about "Negroes." In spite of his cultural "racelessness," the protagonist clearly catches the racial reference and is insulted by it. He begins to leave, but pauses to see in her eccentric face "a flicker of bewilderment, then hard as a stone tablet" (203). "I walked out," the protagonist simply says, presumably for the last time.

He leaves Barnes, however, only physically, as his emotional identification with her character, Robin Vote, becomes the structural frame upon which the remainder of the novel is hung. His final gaze into Djuna Barnes's face, and hers, like a mirror, into his, is like a fulfillment of Matthew O'Connor's prophecy in *Nightwood*—"in the end," he tells Nora Flood, an "observer" whose identity will become intricately intertwined with Robin's, "you'll all be locked together, like the poor beasts that get their antlers mixed and are found dead that way, their heads fattened with a knowledge of each other they never wanted, having had to contemplate each other, head-on and eye to eye, until death" (100). From that moment on, Pinckney's protagonist seems locked together with Barnes, unable to escape her passing racial remark. He throws himself almost immediately into a project to document, and record on index cards, every occasion of literary racism, a search that would resemble Robin's obsessive decadence were it not so pitifully comic. He travels to Europe, much like Robin leaves for America, with a self-destructive woman whose identification with *Nightwood*'s Jenny Petherbridge seems obvious when she tells the protagonist, "This life isn't mine, I'm only squatting in it" (259), and becomes "obsessively" violent. Finally, after he returns to America at his grandfather's death, he finds himself, in the final sequence of the book, inside a church, precisely as Robin does at the end of *Nightwood*, where he wallows in the emotion of self-realization, just as Robin carries on her decadent dance with Nora's dog. Moreover, just as Robin's actions in the chapel indicate an abandonment of her efforts to become human and an acceptance of her natural (animal) state (Frank 49), so it is for the protagonist of *High Cotton* and his reluctant "acceptance" of his racial heritage.

The remarkable component of this parallel journey is that Barnes was able to inspire it in the protagonist not with something she said, but with something she almost said, but didn't. The protagonist clearly heard the near-utterance, "Negro," and Barnes's behavior makes clear she almost said it, but in view of the fact that the "dialogue" was essentially an inferred one, the consequences it provokes may seem exaggerated. On the other hand, the protagonist's histrionic response to the unspoken utterance may, in fact, be connotative of the linguistic subtlety with which the subversion in this work has been executed. As V.N. Volosinov reminds a reader, "There is no reason for saying that meaning belongs to a word as such. In essence, meaning belongs to a word in its position between speakers; that is, meaning is realized only in the process of active, responsive understanding. Meaning does not reside in the word or the soul of the speaker or the soul of the listener" (102). The result, that some are wise to a subversion and others (its targets) are not, is precisely the point of such a literature.

However, this is only the beginning of Pinckney's complex subversion. Even more important than the transparent identification of the protagonist with Robin Vote is the framework into which Pinckney has placed that relationship. Paul Ricoeur, in his work on metaphor, refers to a "second-order reference," an indirect reference that emerges from the foundation of a more direct metaphorical reference (153). It is such a second-order reference upon which Pinckney's fullest meaning is established.

The character of Djuna Barnes in *High Cotton* is designed to elicit thoughts of Robin Vote, who then becomes a metaphor for the protagonist's search for identity while stuck between two opposing worlds. What strikes the knowledgeable Barnes scholar, however, is the remarkable verisimilitude with which Pinckney has endowed the character of Barnes. So precise is it in its detail that nearly everything Pinckney describes can be documented in a memoir by Barnes's closest companion of the time, Hank O'Neal (80–98). What seems clear is that Pinckney's work is intended as a realistic portrayal of Djuna Barnes, not just a character based upon her. On the other hand, it is *not* Barnes, for despite the realistic portrayal, characters in novels are merely the sum of the language used to develop them (Greiner 107). In this case, his language of realism serves to remind readers of its contrast with the modernist, even surrealistic, style of *Nightwood*. The result is that Barnes becomes a "second-order reference," a metaphor for her own writing which, when reshaped and confined by realistic writing, jars the reader with an incongruent and contrapuntal symbiosis that works back upon the more transparent metaphor of Robin Vote, requiring that it now be read as "out-of-place"—in effect, turning it upside down.

As a result, the protagonist's search for identity—comic and picaresque—becomes darker and more frightening. As *Nightwood*'s Matthew O'Connor says of Robin, "our faulty racial memory is fathered by fear. Destiny and history are untidy; we fear memory of that disorder. Robin did not" (118). Robin does not fear memory because she has no memory; she is amoral—both innocent and decadent, child and desperado. The protagonist of *High Cotton* likewise has a faulty racial memory and is driven by fear—at times innocently, at others decadently—to flee the implications of it. Because his constant references to family establish him as the child, he may in the same manner be considered the desperado, running like a fugitive from Djuna Barnes's apartment at her mention of race (203). Where he runs is irrelevant, for it is his past that haunts him, even though, or perhaps because, he is able to recall family incidences in such vivid detail. Those recollections are his prison.

Robin's metaphorical presence in *High Cotton*, then, is clearly dichotomic; she works against the prevailing expectation in *Nightwood*, inasmuch as she represents the antithesis of what it means to be culture-bound, forced by her circumstances to deal with issues precisely because they *are* cultural. She is often evoked as a negative presence—what she is not rather than what she is (Frann 41). Seen against that model, *High Cotton*'s protagonist seems completely culture-bound. Unlike Robin, prevailing expectation renders *him* painfully obtrusive. Taxi drivers pass him by at night; women joggers speed up as if fleeing whenever they see him (193). He counters the obtrusiveness by attempting to hide; he carries a semiotics textbook with him on the subway in an effort to be ignored, or he tries to blend in by working for a black militant organization. He is, one might conclude, a human turning into a beast—a "chameleon," as he calls himself at one point. If Robin is a metaphor for individualism, then *High Cotton*'s protagonist plays against it as the embodiment of conformity, confined, even when he operates in direct contrast to situational expectations, to the parameters by which the culture functions.

This contrapuntal dance eventually becomes the ultimate paradox for Pinckney's protagonist. Lynn DeVore makes a strong case that the characters in *Nightwood* find their roots in autobiographical incidences in Barnes's Paris experience—Robin, for example, is said to be modeled after the eccentric Elsa Loringhoven, who is described in one account with shaved head, black lips, yellow face powder, a canceled postage stamp on each cheek, and a coal scuttle strapped to her head like a helmet (77). So the character of Robin is based on a real woman, yet is so convincingly fictionalized that her search for identity becomes a frightening enterprise from the darkside. Pinckney's protagonist is fictitious, yet is so clearly a representation of the author that the reader is turned into a voyeur. James Scott shows the implications of this paradox for Pinckney by pointing out that the fictional character of the fabulist often appears on the page as a walking, talking abstraction, while the naturalist is forced into portraying the complexities of real people (117). This is exactly the contrast in how *High Cotton*'s protagonist appears to Pinckney's dual audience—fabulistic to the black reader, naturalistic to the white reader. Unless this hypostatic dialogue with the author's white audience is tempered, it overwhelms the pragmatic, or fabulist, reading, and its portrayal of "reality" becomes the lens through which the book must be read. As Buber describes it, "Every real relation...in the world is exclusive. Its *Thou* is freed, steps forth, is single, and confronts you.... This does not mean that nothing else exists; but all else lives in *its* light" (*I and Thou* 78). For the African American author, the "corrective mechanism" is to subvert the white audience's reading of it.

Only one outcome is possible; Richard Eder notes that, in the end, the protagonist, "unable to throw himself into his countrymen's battles and glories, is [*at the same time*] unable to separate himself from them. [*So*] he attends with his oblique view; he participates through estrangement" (8). In *Nightwood*, Robin finds her destiny in an anticultural act of regression, slipping back into bestiality. Her search for identity is ultimately a failure because it struggles against forces deep within the character, where they are difficult to find and, apparently, impossible to alter. *High Cotton*'s protagonist likewise turns regressive, into the past and his Grandfather Eustice, but unlike Robin, moves predictably toward the culturally acceptable, where the result is portrayed, in contrast to Robin's search, as a successful endeavor. "I minded the strict rules of conduct," the protagonist says at the end, "and the tribal code that said that I, as a black, had a responsibility to help my people, to honor the race. Now I am sorry that I went to such lengths not to be of much use to myself just so no one would be able to ask anything of me. To have nothing to offer was not, after all, the best way to have nothing to lose" (306).

This is the point at which the Literature of Subversion teeters most precariously, for most critics would expect the subversion to be exposed by the author in a manner which would allow the author to declare victory over the targets of the subversion—white culture. However, the "last word" does not always mean the "last laugh." In fact, as Bakhtin points out near the end of his own life, the unified "I," in this case the "Black 'I,'" in spite of his or her freedom, cannot change the material world; to portray otherwise would be disingenuous, if not deceptive. What the author *can* change is the *sense* of existence, the way people perceive it, which is why it is sometimes subversive, and why its freedom comes uniquely through the "word" (*Speech Genres* 137–138).

That *High Cotton*'s protagonist now seems committed to fulfilling his destiny as his grandfather's protégé is precisely the ending which readers, both white and black, would expect for this novel—for white readers, because it seems "right"; for black readers, because its cultural conformity seems consistent with the values of the novel. Then again, this is the destination of all effective subversion. The protagonist appears to be a wandering young idealist, so committed to his search for identity that he never even carries along a name. In the end, though, to have donned the identity of his Grandfather Eustice is not, as it appears, a resolution, but a restatement of his original condition. If Grandfather Eustice proudly took his place in a "bright and damn near white" institution (like Harvard University or the Congregationalist Church), thought himself above his black parishioners, and emphasized his Ivy League education, how is the story of *High Cotton*'s protagonist any different? He cannot be said to have discovered an identity; he has only rediscovered his lack of one. As Louis Kannenstine notes, "to call a stop between uncertainties is to perceive man in 'the halt position of the damned,' to halt the flow of experience in order to observe what is lost in custom or in the multiplicity of things" (90). So while Pinckney's white audience might take comfort in having observed a young black man find "success" and his "destiny" in white America, as they would have expected to see, Pinckney can enjoy the real success of his subversive anti-message: search for your identity in white America, and search again, and then again. Then when "high yellow" becomes "high cotton," you're there—"the halt position of the damned."

Chapter 4

The Literature of Vivification

So much has been written on August Wilson's project to chronicle the African American experience through each decade of the twentieth century that the series, which now includes eight plays—*Jitney!* (1979), *Ma Rainey's Black Bottom* (1984), *Fences* (1987), *Joe Turner's Come and Gone* (1988), *The Piano Lesson* (1990), *Two Trains Running* (1992), *Seven Guitars* (1996), and *King Hedley II* (2001)—sometimes seems like a monolith. That effect may be more thematic than theatrical; the plays are rich in their variety of characters and conflicts, and in the resolutions to those conflicts. But beneath the diversity within the dramatic framework of the plays lies the potentially ideological assertion that the present for black America has been thoroughly shaped by a history of race-related stolen opportunity and broken relationships, or what Michael Morales calls "a simultaneously reactive/reconstructive engagement with the representation of blacks and the representation of history by the dominant culture" (105). Traditionally in Wilson's plays, it is the protagonist's personal past that is the lens through which the play's "present" is seen. In *The Piano Lesson*, however, Wilson traces the play's historical complications back three generations, to an incident in the family's slave legacy that has left them to face the present in terms of a history that, seventy-five years later, is not just personal, but communal and familial.

In spite of its flirtations with the myth of slavery, or perhaps because of it, *The Piano Lesson* serves well to illustrate the Literature of

Vivification, an African American literary type in which the author engages in hypostatic dialogue with both black and white audiences. Black literature, like any emerging literary tradition, must balance its legitimacy with the traditional white audience with the expectation that it will keep faith with its emerging black audience. The Literature of Vivification plays its role in that balance by demonstrating African American literature's mastery of accepted literary forms and previous works, or in other words, by proving for both white and black audiences the works' place in the established literary mainstream. The consummate such work of African American literature might be *Invisible Man*, the 1953 novel by Ralph Ellison, but *The Piano Lesson* offers perhaps a better analysis of what the Literature of Vivification is because, in a variety of ways, it bears such close similarities to Toni Morrison's *Beloved*, an important, and obvious, work of mythification, that the differences between the two highlight the distinctive elements of the Literature of Vivification. Both *Beloved* and *The Piano Lesson* examine the legacy of slavery, both contain prominent supernatural elements, both tread around the idea of family myth. Nevertheless, as *The Piano Lesson* will demonstrate, the particulars of theme, content, setting, or even veracity are not the source by which African American literature is classified in this typology, even when those particulars include such staples of the African American myth as slavery, cruel white characters, or supernatural acts.

The momentum of the play is driven by conflict over how best to engage history—as iconographically centered mythology, which, like all myth, would consecrate the *events* of the past, or as foundation for the present, which would seek to fulfill the *promise* of the past. As in Mikhail Bakhtin's analysis of Dostoevsky, the issue here can be framed in terms of epistemology—how to depict an idea while retaining its broader relevance. Bakhtin writes:

> The idea lives not in one person's isolated individual consciousness—if it remains there only it degenerates and dies. The idea begins to live,…to develop, to find and renew its verbal expression, to give birth to new ideas, only when it enters into genuine dialogic relationships with other ideas, with the ideas of others. Human thought becomes genuine thought, that is, an idea, only under conditions of living contact with an alien thought, a thought embodied in someone else's voice, that is, in someone else's consciousness expressed in discourse. At that point…the idea is born and lives. (*Problems* 88)

For Wilson, as for Bakhtin, the truth is to be found in the polyphonic chorus of contradictory ideas which are brought to bear on the search for an answer (*Problems* 20). The fulcrum of this polyphony is the piano. Boy Willie, the great-grandson of the slave whose art graces the piano, has come north to Pittsburgh to claim his half of the piano, which is currently in the possession of his sister, Berniece. He is a ruffian, and feels that the proceeds from the sale of the piano offer him his best chance to escape the economic and social oppression that has burdened the men in his family since slavery. His dream of escape is blunted, however, by Berniece's unwillingness to sell what is, for her, a sacred icon of the family's sacrificial legacy. The result is that Wilson has redefined the frustration of carrying the burden of the past, which is at the center of his other plays, into a question of how best to utilize the past. Throughout the play, then, the piano becomes a touchstone by which antithetical attitudes about the past may be evaluated. None of those attitudes should be assumed to be Wilson's monologistic pronouncement; the dialogue over the piano so effectively engages the reader, or theatergoer, white and black, that it ultimately becomes a dialogue over the text itself. Boy Willie, in his attempts at understanding, hears Berniece, Doaker, Lyman, Wining Boy, even Sutter; the reader hears all those voices, too, and Boy Willie's, and each other's (including Wilson's) as well.

The dialogue is brought into focus at the point in the play where Doaker—Boy Willie and Berniece's uncle—tells Boy Willie's friend Lyman why Berniece refuses to sell the piano (40–46). He relates the story of his grandfather's carvings on the piano in a tale so imbued with rich images of bondage, acceptance, and retribution, that it seems to have been handed down, parent-to-child, detail by detail, since the time of its origin. It is, in other words, the family slave narrative. For Boy Willie, however, the dynamic of enslavement is not just a product of oral tradition; the events of his own life constitute, in his mind, a second, metaphorical, enslavement—economic, not physical—from which he attempts a desperate flight to freedom through the acquisition of James Sutter's land, upon which his family had worked as slaves, and which would offer him, for the first time in his life, a substantial degree of achievement and self-realization. Arnold Rampersad identifies such a pursuit of self-realization as an inherent feature of the slave narrative (105), so that the play itself comes to constitute a broader, metaphorical slave narrative, being lived out by Boy Willie and his search for economic freedom.

The structure of the play, then, is a narrative within a narrative, a literal slave narrative integrated into a metaphorical one, with the latter (Boy Willie's narrative) reflecting both a continuation of and an attempt to bring to fruition the former one (the family's). The success of Boy Willie's narrative is dependent upon reaching a shared understanding of the traditional family narrative, the one related by Doaker, so that the interchange between the two narratives becomes a form of what Buber calls a "meeting," a relationship so dialogical that it takes on a hypostasis, or in Buber's words, "the gates are united in one gateway of real life, and you no longer know through which you have entered" (*I and Thou* 102). Such a meeting is the essence of the Literature of Vivification, and occurs when the reader, or theatergoer (both white *and* black), arrives at the point at which the play's (or novel's) "truth" is posited and feels that he or she put it there, even when such "truth" is, *in posse*, at odds with what the author intended. This is the essence of a hypostatic relationship between author and reader. In *The Piano Lesson*, Wilson establishes the potential for such a hypostasis by abdicating the monologistic authorial voice and creating a polyphony of voices, each reminding the reader that truth "is born between people collectively searching for truth, in the process of their dialogic interaction" (*Problems* 110). One voice consists of a slave narrative that has been carved into the body of the piano; a second voice is in Boy Willie's response, an improvised effort to translate that myth into the reality of his own economic and social emancipation.

The transition would be easier for Boy Willie if the narratives were better integrated, so that one narrative does not get destroyed by the preeminence of the other. However, the interaction in *The Piano Lesson* is instead structured like the classic dialogue; the two narratives are linear—evolutionary rather than integrated—extending "into the boundless past and the boundless future" (*Speech Genres* 170), and so, in the manner of the traditional dialogical pattern, the direction of the interaction is not toward monologistical resolution or mere progress toward such a goal, but toward an appropriate dialogical truth. The result is an ever-changing series of recreations of the myth, in which the narrative gets repeated in a different version every time, each with its own veracity (Byerman 7).

This is what Wilson has managed to accomplish in *The Piano Lesson*. Boy Willie is never able to take charge of his own narrative; every move he makes in his attempt to escape the legacy with which he has been left is made in dialogue with the mythology of the piano. Even his final desperate attempt to defy the myth and steal the piano is frustrated, and he is forced, finally, into acquiring his freedom and self-realization in the emotional realm, not the economic one, by confronting Sutter's ghost instead of buying his land. What Wilson demands, then, is that the theatergoer understand the ultimate importance of the slave narrative depicted on the piano in authenticating Boy Willie's metaphorical slave narrative, and how, because of the linear nature of the relationship, the family myth must be destroyed, or his own narrative altered, to create a new one.

Wilson posits, then, a complex, universal way of looking at black history, and does so by structuring *The Piano Lesson* on three tiers. First, he creates a play within a play by describing a mythological slave narrative carved into the play's focal object, an old piano, and repeated several times by the play's characters. Second, he uses the piano and its attendant narrative as a haunting presence around which dialogue may occur, as a symbol for the truth which Boy Willie, in his quest for self-realization, must discover if he is to achieve that goal. Finally, he juxtaposes Boy Willie's undertaking with that of his slave ancestors, and makes his quest an extension of theirs, so that Boy Willie's story, and the play itself, becomes a metaphorical slave narrative in its own right.

Certainly, while Boy Willie is not a *literal* runaway slave, his flight to Pittsburgh bears all the earmarks of the journey his ancestors would have taken a century before. He has come North, just across the Ohio River, seeking not only economic and social freedom, but to reclaim the heritage built by his ancestors and stolen from him. He even seems to be pursued by a sort of spiritual slavecatcher. His chief dissimilarity with the runaway slave would appear to be his inability to persuade anyone on the merits of his plan; the myth is "dead," relegated to monologistic retelling and not dialogical search. What he surrenders in the absence of authority, however, he reacquires with single-mindedness—he is determined to take the piano regardless of Berniece's opinion or threats. This quality of being "driven" clearly places *The Piano Lesson* within the conventions of an established literary motif—the "running man," the outcast who is fleeing the culture of which he is nominally a part, but in which he is the outsider: the American immigrant from Europe at the turn of the century, the pioneer in the westward expansion, the runaway slave (Klotman 17).

So in spite of its transparent black trappings, *The Piano Lesson* is deeply ingrained in traditional literary forms. Perhaps for that reason, the issue of slavery does not create, for the white audience, the pragmatic reading that would lead to an ideological interpretation, which would signify a work of inversion. Far from it, in fact. In the same manner in which the play uses parallel slave narratives to complicate a reader's interpretation of the events, so too does it use parallel dialogues to "complicate" the search of truth (in contrast with the monological works of mythification, which make truth simple and obvious to everyone). Wilson engages the reader, or theatergoer, precisely as Boy Willie engages Berniece, and the instability of their common search for a truth which only the piano can convey is matched by the instability with which the reader, black or white, is engaged by Wilson in the author-reader joint search for truth.

The result can only be vivifying. As Bakhtin makes plain, the search for truth is a dialogical enterprise, soliciting a polyphony of voices in its search. However, what is often less clear, particularly in a work as motivated by ideas as this one, is that what Bakhtin calls "truth" is never just a destination, an unambiguous and indisputable (and monologistic) end product of a dialogistic quest. Instead, the end product about which the search for truth is undertaken is dialogical from its beginning, in that a "reading" of a social text cannot be considered identical with the text itself. The key point, then, is not just that opposing forms of understanding come into contact with one another in the *making* of dialogue, but that the "truth" itself is predisposed to dialogical auto-activity, self-contradiction, the capability to be reinterpreted even as it is being interpreted (*Problems* 92–94, 126). As a result, whatever truth emerges for a specific reader from *The Piano Lesson* will always be unstable, even upon subsequent readings by the same reader.

Certainly, the paradigm of the slave narrative is not without a certain amount of monologistical baggage. The purpose for the antebellum slave narrative was to help the slave remember the life from which he or she had fled (Stepto 1). Deep within each such narrative, then, is the psychological empowerment for self-identity and linguistic authority, a vehicle through which the former slave might construct an apologetic for his or her own personality in terms of a response to the South's "peculiar institution." By doing so, it gave the former slave an opportunity to reconstruct his or her psychological health.[1] For Frederick Douglass, identity was rooted in the courage to design and execute a flight to freedom; for Booker T. Washington, it was in explaining how slavery had taught behaviors and attitudes to its victims that were subsequently making them successful in postbellum America. In every case for such a narrative, the bondage is shown ultimately to have served the interests of the one who had been subjected to it and subsequently escaped it.

No one seems to need such a psychological reconstruction any worse than Boy Willie. He is essentially a rogue—a "survivor" who has learned, in the process of surviving, to steal, cheat, and lie, and who now sees his chance to emerge from the cycle that has killed more of the men in his family than he wishes to remember. His passionate denial of any responsibility for Crawley's death in the face of Berniece's accusations make that clear (52). Nevertheless, the accusations themselves remind Boy Willie of just how far he has come in the family legacy, and how close he is to escaping it through the piano. The fact that he now needs the piano, the hard evidence of the legacy, with the likeness of his ancestors carved into the wood itself, to complete his journey is ironic evidence that his identity will forever be, for better or worse, intertwined with the past. For Boy Willie, however, stories of the family's courage in saving this icon are no longer sufficient for the maintenance of his own self-concept. He is left, then, with seeking to establish his own slave narrative, even a metaphorical one, to do for himself what Doaker's narrative has done for the rest of the family—communicate a mythology of black authority and potential to succeed within the confines of, and by the rules of, a white world. The narrative has worked for previous generations because of the piano; it has served as the touchstone by which members of the family could reinforce their belief in the legacy, regardless of how far they roamed from it. Wilson suggests this in Doaker's story of the trains. They go in all directions, Doaker says, and many people assume they can arrive at their destinations by going in any direction, but in the end, the train always returns (18–19). Boy Willie and Wining Boy's simultaneous arrival in Pittsburgh reinforces a certain truth in the metaphor; to this point, Boy Willie's life has reflected this "restless wandering" of the freed slave experience (Pereira 1). For Boy Willie, however, the escape from white domination is more ambitious, and he seeks a change from which the train will never return (90–92). The irony is that he must use the piano to accomplish such a change, to authenticate his identity, just as every male in his family has done since its construction. The difference is that rather than discovering his identity in the piano's layering of myth, he must do so by demythologizing it, or precisely what a white reader must do with the play's mythology in order to achieve a hypostatic reading.

Boy Willie's actions seem to fall logically within an evolutionary series of phases through which the slave narrative, as a traditional black literary form embraced by whites, has passed. Robert Stepto writes that slave narratives develop in three phases, each building upon the social and psychological dynamic of the previous stage. The first phase he calls the "eclectic phase," in which the evidence for authenticating the narrative is appended to the tale, and comes from outside the tale itself. The earliest slave narratives bore affidavits signed by white editors, writers, or slaveholders, stating that the witness knew personally that the slave was capable of writing, and had in fact written, the narrative to which the affidavit was attached. In the second phase, the "integrated phase," the authenticating evidence became integrated into the tale and became one or more voices within the tale, albeit no less monological. This appears to be the phase in which Doaker's narrative of the family legacy of the piano exists. It is replete with mythological elements, specific names and places and events, all of which serve to bear witness, through their connection with established fact, to the tale's "truth," or authenticity (though it may be important to notice that this tale, as with all such myths, is interfused with enough contradictions that it may *not* be "authentic," in the sense of having occurred in the literal manner the narrative details). As such, it becomes the core of what Patricia Gantt calls their "shared southernness" (79). Boy Willie seems to have moved to the third phase, the "generic phase" of the slave narrative, during which it becomes no longer necessary to add details merely to authenticate the narrative; the narrative itself takes total precedence, subsuming all other authenticating documents or strategies (Stepto 4–6). At this point, the narrative stands on its own merit.

This appears to be the point at which Boy Willie is attempting his escape from the family legacy. His own life is no longer authenticated by the piano and its mythological connection to the past. His only rationale for keeping the piano lies in Berniece putting it to some practical use—giving lessons. In the absence of that, he himself is willing to put it to use.[2] However, his identity is no longer based in the mythology it represents. This is the significant point in Stepto's typology; at this point, the narrative becomes a generic one—it can be anyone's story, or to be more dialogically precise, everyone's story. The myth for Boy Willie no longer demands that *anyone* keep the piano; all that is demanded is a willingness to follow in the tradition of the myth, and to do whatever it takes to succeed, just as those who carved the piano, maintained it, and subsequently stole it for the family demonstrated. He becomes, in Pamela Jean Monaco's words, a "living reminder" of his family's past (95).

One of Wilson's important distinctives in the play, and certainly an important component for understanding the dialogical search, is the difference between Boy Willie and Berniece. Each has an understanding of the world that demonstrates a certain nobility of vision, but their understanding of each other's visions is so limited that they seem, at times, not to have shared the same heritage. Indeed, for whatever reason, they have arrived at different spiritual destinations. Slave narratives are essentially *Bildungsroman*, and like the typical *Bildungsroman*, slave narratives often fail to distinguish adequately between male and female development. *The Piano Lesson* could conceivably have told Berniece's story—the attempt of a strong woman to save the family myth and heritage from a brother who would sell it away. That would have required a greater investment on Wilson's part into "eclectic phase" narratives, along with the accompanying authenticating strategies—in this case, the rich detail of the story, the ghosts who seem to confirm it, the fascinating almost-mythic qualities to the narrative. This might have had the effect of mythification, tying the play even closer to African American tradition, for in black literature, history often assumes a mythic quality, or in some cases even a mythified quality, in order to respond to questions of identity raised by a history largely told by and focusing on whites. The result is a black American history structured as an ongoing mythified relationship between the living and the dead (Morales 106).

Consider, for example, the accidental deaths of the white men being attributed to the Ghosts of the Yellow Dog. Certainly, the explanations for the deaths the reader hears in the play are not the explanations that would be offered by the families of the victims, or by the mass media. The explanations offered are mythical explanations, serving to authenticate the lives of the men who died and became the Ghosts (just as Boy Willie seeks authentication through ownership of Sutter's land), and they serve to authenticate the sacredness of the piano itself—it was important enough for black men to die for, and it was important enough for white men to kill for. Berniece believes in the mythical power of the piano and acknowledges it as a point of contact with her ancestral heritage; this explains her absolute reluctance to sell it—it *was* important enough to die for (but only within the parameters of the myth). The result is an acknowledgment of the symbiotic relationship between her generation and those that came before—for mutual gain or mutual destruction—just as in the African ancestral rituals that were the source of the original myth (Morales 109). She turns to those ancestors during the family confrontation with Sutter's ghost near the end of the play.

One of the strengths of such a mythology is its ability to empower the believer—particularly given its power to define the past and to define reality. It was precisely for this reason that slave narratives and slave songs became such an important literary form for black America. Such narratives take control of the environment by shaping it sympathetically, and in doing so, giving individuals control over themselves and their destiny (Dixon 20). As a result, then, it is generally insignificant whether the myth bears the whole truth, or any truth at all. Quite frequently, slave narratives were shaped and reshaped by abolitionists who wanted to convey a specific political message. In *The Piano Lesson*, the truth of the narrative is subsumed by its communal and familial empowerment. Consider the empowering effect achieved by Wining Boy's retelling of the Yellow Dog myth: "I done been to where the Southern cross the Yellow Dog and called out their names. They talk back to you, too....I can't say how they talked to nobody else. But to me it just filled me up in a strange sort of way to be standing there on that spot. I didn't want to leave. It felt like the longer I stood there the bigger I got" (34–35). Doaker's retelling of the piano myth offers the same sense of power (40–46).

What is not so obvious is that Doaker's narrative bears internal evidence of its literal inauthenticity. In documenting the family heritage, he relates that Old Berniece and her son Charles (Doaker's and Charles's father) were sold as payment for the piano to a slaveholder "down in Georgia" (42). In his grief over their departure (and in response to the white mistress's grief over losing her favorite slave), the first Boy Willie (Doaker's grandfather) carved their portraits, as well as much of the family history, into the piano. What seems problematic about this genealogy is that Doaker's and Charles's father would have been in Georgia, apparently some distance away, when these statues were being carved, and was unlikely to have known anything about them, or that they even existed. That becomes important when Doaker relates that his father, Charles, becomes obsessed enough with the piano to raid the Sutter farm and steal it, an act that would lead directly to his death. Enslaved in Georgia, he would likely not even have known about the piano, much less become obsessed with it. Nevertheless, as though authenticating the myth, even Sutter's grandson becomes complicit in it, appearing like what Anne Fleche calls "the vampire from some expressionistic film" to take his revenge on those, like Boy Willie, who will not believe the myth, and who will not acknowledge his existence (9).

It is clear, though, that the myth has sustained Berniece to the present, and it is her faith in the myth that ultimately resolves the conflict over the piano, though she treats the myth throughout the play with a selective reverence. She refuses to play the piano, and has done so ever since her mother's death (70), as a way of forgetting the past—of keeping the spirits from "walking around...the house" (70)—even as she honors its sacredness. Likewise, she denies the existence of the Ghosts of the Yellow Dog (15, 34), though she is ultimately forced to acknowledge both the past and the spirits in reclaiming her faith in the myth, when she plays the piano and furiously calls on her ancestors to help Boy Willie defeat the ghost of Sutter in a final showdown. It is a polyphonic, heteroglottic moment, demonstrating once and for all, for the characters in the play, the instability of the family myth, and for the reader, the dialogical nature of the search for the meaning of history. For the family myth, it is a landmark moment, and a reconciling one, for as the play's ending seems to indicate, both Berniece and Boy Willie seem to have forgotten, or are willing to moderate, the context out of which their dialogue produced such an outcome (Werner 46). As a result, the play moves away from mythification and becomes rooted in its characters and their personal growth—in vivification.

For the reader, the response to the text is much the same. It is as if, in Buber's words, the reader no longer knows which gateway to truth he or she has entered. As Bakhtin conveys it, "At any moment in the development of the dialogue there are immense, boundless masses of forgotten contextual meanings, but at certain moments...they are recalled and invigorated in renewed form....Nothing is absolutely dead; every meaning will have its homecoming festival" (*Speech Genres* 170). It is as if the reader, having followed Boy Willie's quest for dialogical understanding with Berniece, has in fact been living his or her own quest for dialogue with the text, and resolves it with the same "forgotten contextual meanings." Boy Willie embarks on his quest for meaning by attempting to purchase the very land that his family had been forced to work as slaves, and working it himself for his own profit. The cost of such self-realization is high—he must surrender the concept of community, the folklore of family, and the respect of his ancestors to acquire the means to his sense of selfhood. He must, in contrast to the reader of the play, reject the possibility of resolving his search through hypostatic dialogue.

For him, then, the decision becomes a *pragmatic* one—the piano has gone untouched by Berniece since Mama Ola died seven years before (10). His argument places him squarely in the tradition of later slave narratives, which had come to view even slavery itself from an increasingly pragmatic perspective (Andrews 64). Nevertheless, it is more than mere pragmatism that sets Boy Willie's story apart as a classic "slave narrative." He was, after all, extremely pragmatic when he was still playing the part of the rogue; skimming wood for himself from the load he was hauling for a white man, as pragmatic as the decision may have seemed, was the catalytic event in Crawley's death. What sets Boy Willie apart is that, like the hero of any *Bildungsroman*, he is moving from the somewhat idyllic world of an almost childlike ignorance, symbolized by his having recently come out of the rural South (a traditional metaphor for innocence and simplicity), into a metaphoric wilderness, just as dark and full of surprises as the ones his ancestors would have faced in *their* escape attempts (Smith 33).

The only obstacle to completing his journey is the material worth he possesses in the piano, a value that stands in contrast to the inherent transcendent and mythic value it possesses for Berniece (51). To liquidate the piano would be to demythologize it, to profane it, to take away the hypostasis of self-identity which Berniece has bestowed upon it, the same self-identity that she placed so completely in Crawley, who seemingly foreshadowed this loss by being taken from her, in her mind, by Boy Willie. In that sense, Boy Willie, by selling the piano, would be asserting the preeminence of his own narrative over that of the piano and its carvings—present over past, utility over tradition, freedom over community, mythification over myth-making. It is, in fact, mythification at its consummate level, an attempt to make his own myth into everyone's myth. At that point, he would be seizing control over the text of his own narrative, a text that most slave narratives, even the one represented by the piano, surrendered to the communal myth-making demands of authentication and audience (Stepto 16–17). Certainly control over the text of bondage is no guarantee of freedom, but it would seem, to Boy Willie, to be evidence of that freedom.

Boy Willie's desire for Sutter's farm is, however, no less mythological than the piano, akin to Jewish or Christian beliefs in a "promised land" or Muslim beliefs regarding Mecca. Ralph Ellison writes, "If we don't know where we are, we have little chance of knowing who we are....If we confuse the time, we confuse the place; and...when we confuse these we endanger our humanity, both physically and morally" (*Shadow* 74). Owning Sutter's land would give Boy Willie that sense of place, of humanity, of identity. It was, after all, he who planned all along to return to the South, that metaphorical wilderness of bondage, while Lyman was staying in Pittsburgh (3). Meanwhile, Doaker, already in Pittsburgh, would continue to ride the trains in every direction as a Pullman Porter (18–19). Doaker, literally a man without a place, is not coincidently the heir who has given up his own claim on the piano, metaphorically renouncing any stake to his own identity, even one based in an authenticated narrative like the piano (69).

In the end, the piano will not authenticate Boy Willie's search for freedom. When he goes to move it, to take possession of it, to claim power over it, the piano will not move (83). It is as if the piano, the text of Boy Willie's and Berniece's competing efforts at mythification, will not allow itself to be mythified. By doing so, it resists becoming Wilson's "icon of slavery" in what could lead to the same sort of mythification for the text itself. "In what way," Bakhtin writes, "would it enrich the [literary] event if [the author] merged with the [reader], and instead of two there would be now only one?"

> And what would I myself gain by the other's merging with me? If he did, he would see and know no more than what I see and know myself; he would merely repeat in himself that want of any issue out of itself which characterizes my own life. Let him rather remain outside of me, for in that position he can see and know what I myself do not see and do not know from my own place, and he can essentially enrich the event of my own life. (*Art and Answerability* 87)

As a result of the piano's (and the play's) resistance to mythification, Boy Willie is forced into dialogue (portrayed in the play as a battle) with the one thing that may still hold authoritative power over his narrative—Sutter's Ghost. Whether he had killed Sutter, as Berniece believes (15), or whether Sutter has taken a position as representative of the whole white world directly in Boy Willie's path, the result is that Boy Willie must confront the myth, ascend the stairs—symbolically "go to the mountaintop"—and defeat this final obstacle to the truth he seeks. He had imagined all along that the piano was his final hurdle, now he finds this engagement with Sutter, which he has desired economically throughout the play, to be his "baptism by fire"—"baptism" implied by his reference to water (105), "fire" by his reference to Hell (105).

This was the point at which the play originally ended; once Boy Willie engaged the ghosts of the past, he had cleared the very hurdle for which he sought to sell the piano (Shannon 149–50). For Wilson, struggle with such ghosts of the past is a real phenomenon for black America, and the ambiguity of outcome a thought-provoking reflection of reality. With Lloyd Richards's guidance, Wilson rewrote his ending. Once on the mountaintop, Boy Willie finds in his dialogical engagement with Sutter's ghost the identity he has long sought, no longer in need of an authenticating "myth." He returns from the conflict ready to grant the validity of the past, tempered by its utility in the present—"if you and Maretha don't keep playing that piano…ain't no telling…me and Sutter both liable to be back" (108). He leaves Pittsburgh no richer (with the exception of the proceeds from watermelons he has brought with him), but wiser; no longer completely disdainful of that which his ancestors loved, no longer completely trusting in his own pursuits. He has, it appears, discovered his hypostasis.

At this point, the parallel narratives come together in a single vision of the future. The effect of such a polyphony of voices arriving at a still-dialogical resolution is to create the same symphony of relationships among the characters as Wilson creates with his dual audiences. He draws near to one, distances himself from the other, back and forth, playing at times with myth, at times with traditional literary conventions, still at other times on deeply human emotions that unify readers of all races, still yet at other times portraying situations that equalize readers and characters in sympathetic feeling, all the while using language that subtly reminds both black and white readers of the reality of social inequality. Ultimately, for both black and white readers, it is the characters who live, are vivified, and not Wilson's ideas or words. In his struggle with the ghosts of the past, he has reached a new level of hypostasis with which a reader, white or black, can identify, and has taken the family's understanding of its shared slave narrative to its final, communal "generic" phase; now both he and Berniece may continue the narrative. Neither of them seeks, nor needs, any further mythification.

Chapter 5

The Literature of Mythification

One of the four channels through which an emerging literary tradition balances its legitimacy with both a traditional audience as well as an emerging one is in the production of literary works which recount (or create) a "shared myth" within a milieu which transcends the question of the works' place in the established literary mainstream. Nevertheless, the beatification of a written discourse is seldom just a result of popular belief or critical praise. Mythification requires the assertion of authority by the African American author, and not everyone assents to that authority, particularly those who might examine the claim most closely. As with the sacred texts of established religions, the creation of a work of mythification is not only a function of the text itself—which, because it is static, acontextual, and monologistic, inferentially claims the authoritative voice necessary for mythification—but of its receptivity, or more accurately, the testimony on its behalf by readers and "critics" who reject and vilify attempts to subject the text to what Bakhtin calls "answerability," or the potential that a reader might engage in a revisionary understanding of it (*Art and Answerability* 276–85). The result often demands, then, a beatification of both text and author; Toni Morrison is the consummate such author, and *Beloved*, the consummate text.

The Literature of Mythification often deals with issues which, by themselves, would constitute what might be considered African American mythology, and slavery would be the supreme example, but the issues themselves are secondary to the literary dynamic by which the author is able to convey the myth to his or her dual audience. The author of works of mythification engages the reader, both black *and* white, pragmatically, at the level of social consequences, or social reality, resulting in a work of literature which seems to prioritize, in Martin Buber's words, "ideas, foreknowledge, and fancy." It uses race not as a point of engagement, but as a source of identification. It engages the reader at the intellectual level, encouraging detached observation, and it invites the reader to bring preexisting extratextual attitudes which might be acted upon by the text, making the literature, at its most extreme, monologic in its voice. This is not, however, a liability for the Literature of Mythification, but an asset, for the Herculean task of such a literature is to explain, as myths are designed to do, the values and idiosyncrasies by which a culture defines itself, and to interpret its members' attitudes and behaviors to the broader world. The result is that the Literature of Mythification transcends the very issues it appears to be addressing and creates an authoritative mythology through which the emerging tradition and the established tradition come together to project a common literary future.

The mythification of Morrison's work began long before *Beloved*. Inspired perhaps by the racial dialect and stereotyped ghetto setting of her first novel, *The Bluest Eye* (1970), reviewers focused on issues of prejudice, hatred, violence, and antisocial behavior, as though the book were a sociological treatise. One reviewer even recommended the book to "social caseworkers" (Marvin 3806). The publisher clearly established the possibility of such a reading by describing the novel as a "stark first novel [that] portrays…one wretched girl growing up poor, black, and ugly—but with a beautiful dream" (*Publisher's Weekly* 3). At least one critic confessed to thinking the attention the book received was excessive and politically motivated. Sara Blackburn writes:

> In 1970, when Toni Morrison's first novel, *The Bluest Eye*, appeared, she reaped the benefits of a growing, middle-class women's movement that was just beginning to acknowledge the reality of its black and poor sisters. As a result, her novel probably attracted more attention than it might otherwise have in the publishing industry and was received rather uncritically by readers and reviewers. (1)

Critics often seemed to misread the novel as a work of inversion; Sara

Blackburn went on to suggest that Morrison could potentially "take her place among the most serious, important, and talented American novelists" only if her writing became more universal in its subject matter, or as she put it, acquired more "stinging immediacy." What critics overlooked at this stage in Morrison's career is the complexity of vision that seemed already to be experimenting with mythification. Perhaps the most unforgettable component of *The Bluest Eye* is a series of readings from the ubiquitous Dick and Jane primers of the 1950s which grow increasingly chaotic with each rendition, losing capitalization, punctuation, and finally spaces between words. As Hurston did with *Dust Tracks on the Road* (1942), Morrison uses code-shifting as a tool for myth-making, expurgating the white text while concurrently, and silently, constructing the black (Furman 20). The readings serve to remind the audience with each rendering that the idealized, sanitized myth of white childhood consummately represented in American society by Dick and Jane contains an implicit contrast with the violent stereotype of black childhood. It is a pragmatic rendering of both cultures that neither would embrace.

Ultimately, Morrison's mythification of African American culture, which would become much more transparent in later works, would be rooted in just such a reversal of almost every expectation the reader would bring to Morrison's portrayal of race.[1] In fact, the consequences, always stunningly unexpected, of black America's engagement with white America, focusing especially on the African wellspring of the American Negro, would become increasingly important to Morrison's vision of literature. Twenty years into her career, she would outline that vision more systematically in *Playing in the Dark* (1992). This "Africanist presence," she writes, is "both a visible and invisible mediating force" in a reader's engagement with literature (47). The use of language to achieve that goal was essential to Morrison as early as her first novel; she points to the complexity with which its opening sentence—"Quiet as it's kept, there were no marigolds in the fall of 1941"—manifests linguistic codes embedded in black culture that convey both the myth and duality of the work right from this point of entry into it (Morrison, "Unspeakable" 218–21). The information given in that opening sentence, she writes, "is a secret between us and a secret that is being kept from us....In order to fully comprehend that position, one needs to think of the immediate political climate during which the writing took place, 1965–1969, during great social upheaval in the life of black people. The…writing was the disclosure of secrets, secrets 'we' shared and those withheld from us by ourselves and by the world outside our community" (218).

Her second novel, *Sula* (1973), manifests deep roots within the Literature of Mythification. It focuses on two women, one metaphorically white (conservative, ordered, mannered, conforming), the other metaphorically black (frivolous, chaotic, unpredictable, iconoclastic). They, and the other women in their lives, are revealed to the audience as agents of social consequences—drowning a little boy, breaking up marriages, killing a child rather than have him grow up enslaved to his manhood—or perhaps more precisely, agents of racial mythology. In what is certainly the book's most stunning example of such mythification, at the climax of *Sula*, the villainy of the metaphorical black character (Sula herself) is revealed to have been the source of stability, morality, and vitality for the entire community.

Song of Solomon (1977), Morrison's third novel, is deeply, and transparently, imbued with African American mythology, opening with a cryptic, but clearly symbolic, reference to the African American myth of the flying Africans—"The North Carolina Mutual Life Insurance agent promised to fly from Mercy to the other side of Lake Superior at three o'clock."—and concluding with the protagonist's avouchment of the myth's transcendental, even perhaps literal, truth—"For now he knew what Shalimar knew: If you surrendered to the air, you could *ride* it." Within the frame of those two attempts at flight exists a world defined by the contrasting worldviews of Macon Dead, a materialistic social climber who is indeed "making dead" every person enslaved (like he is) by western values, and his sister Pilate, an American griot whose physical and emotional characteristics elevate her into the novel's spiritual center, or what one critic called "a continuum of self-actualization" (Samuels 61). The pilgrim on this metaphorical Afro-American journey to salvation is Milkman Dead, so named because he has suckled far too long at his biological mother's breast. It is his symbolic suckling from his spiritual mother Pilate which brings him not only maturity, but community, through an understanding of and commitment to the communal heritage borne of his people's rejection of their enslavement by the west and western values. In a remarkable comment on the novel's penchant toward mythification, Reynolds Price called it "a wise and spacious novel," [lifted] "on the wide slow wings of human sympathy, well-informed wit and the rare plain power to speak wisdom to other human beings" (1).

Morrison, just a year before *Song of Solomon*'s publication, had deflected criticism from the black community (who were likely reading the novels as works of subversion, with their sometimes unsympathetic, or even unrealistic, portrayals of black characters) regarding the manner in which she portrays the characters in her novels, and voiced her commitment to exploring the myths of the black experience critically, without regard to what whites might think (Jordan 113). To do otherwise, some thought, would be to risk a cultural imperialism that colonizes black writers for its own purpose (Wisker, "Disremembered" 81). Nellie McKay posits that, given *Song of Solomon*'s male protagonist and mythic quest, both black and white audiences were finally beginning, by 1981, to acknowledge Morrison's mythification of black culture, and that *Tar Baby*'s (1981) use of white characters further gave white audiences "themes and patterns with which they could identify" (5, 6).

Beloved, published six years after *Tar Baby* and with a graphic portrayal of the horrors of slavery, would risk all she had accomplished. Morrison's rising popularity had begun to foreground her themes of mythification, and, once exposed, just as with all "sacred" literature (i.e., literature which attempts to speak authoritatively, or in Bakhtin's terms, monologistically), critics resistant to the myth begin attacking not only the literature, but the myth as well. Certainly, the politics of race, intersected by a novel so transparent in its mythification, raised the stakes for Morrison and her critics beyond what anyone might have thought possible.

That Morrison's work was now being acknowledged for its mythification was obvious in an extraordinarily venomous review of *Beloved* by Stanley Crouch, in which he criticizes her work as a constant series of ideological commercials, and criticizes Morrison herself for doing whatever she thinks necessary in the pursuit of success. He believes Morrison has produced just another piece of "protest pulp fiction" that he identifies closely with certain African American writings (likely works of inversion, but perhaps works of mythification as well). By accusing her of exploiting racial stereotypes and simplistic explanations for African

American social history, he tries to take critical opinion of her work in a whole new direction. He calls *Beloved* a "blackface holocaust novel" whose sole purpose is to ensure Morrison's success in "the big-time martyr ratings contest" (40). Crouch's review would have been uncomfortable even if its only flaw was its lack of civility, but the scope of its accusations, targeting both myth and myth-maker, implies that Morrison's success is undeserved and constitutes an attempt by the literary establishment to remedy past injustices by legitimating, or even venerating, an emerging racial mythology.

Contemporary scholarship has often identified such views among literary critics who presumably harbor parochial expectations of literature and react with racist condemnation whenever a minority work violates those expectations. Among such critics, value judgments are made on the basis of a proscribed standard of black behavior established by white society. The result, Aribert Schroeder writes, is that black fiction is analyzed from a white perspective, and any work that seems to deal with oppression is understood as "protest literature," which will always be judged too "narrow" and "one-sided" to meet the standards of "mainstream literature" (Schroeder 110–11). However accurate this depiction may be, it seems to describe a reaction, like Crouch's, to Morrison's fiction misread as a work of inversion, which is precisely how white audiences have, at times, interpreted Morrison's fiction.

As a result of the racial politics Morrison's work was engendering, the prospect of her literary beatification, especially manifested in critical reaction to *Beloved*, became an issue of public debate later that year. When *Beloved* failed to win the National Book Award, forty-eight African American writers, including many of her former protégés, signed an open letter to *The New York Times Book Review* questioning why Morrison had never won the National Book Award or the Pulitzer Prize (Atlas 45). The statement addresses the issue in concepts that echo Schroeder, suggesting that James Baldwin was ignored for any major literary prize because of his race and that Toni Morrison was being subjected to the same treatment. The effort was of such scope that it appeared to many, including Ralph Ellison, to be a bald-faced and inappropriate campaign for literary lionization for Morrison. Even so, the publicity from the controversy served to consolidate her momentum with the critics. Shortly thereafter, she won the Pulitzer Prize and was a finalist for the prestigious Ritz Hemingway Prize in Paris. Two years later, she won Italy's most prestigious literary award, the Chianti Ruffino Antico Fattore Award. Three years later came the Nobel Prize.

Beloved, like other works of mythification, engages the reader, both black and white, pragmatically, at the level of social (rather than personal) consequences, so that the novel ultimately seems to be driven by, as Buber would say, "ideas, foreknowledge, and fancy," and feels, especially through its most extreme episodes, monologic. For example, when Sethe, Denver, and Beloved, late in the story, harmonize in a series of parallel internal monologues, their justifications are fraught with such incoherent logic ("if I hadn't killed her, she would have died"), startling overstatement ("She cut my head off every night"), and linguistic curiosities ("I am standing in the rain falling I am not taken") that, when the three merge finally into antiphonal poetry, the result is something between a soliloquy and a sermon, but nothing that seems designed to engage a reader of either race in dialogue (246–67). The section accomplishes its monologism not only by defying a literal reading—three people rarely engage in conversational thought, even if one of them is a ghost—and by positing a racial mythology uncomfortable to both black or white readers, but by, instead, foregrounding language, using the inherent precariousness of the signifier to create enough authorial distance from the reader to demand a reader's assent to the myth.

The place *Beloved* has come to occupy as the consummate work in Morrison's dossier comes as no surprise, then, to anyone watching the evolution of her beatification; the novel conflates the themes of mythification which appear both so powerfully and yet so antipathetic and transparent in her earlier works. The novel foregrounds the pathology of slavery in a way that allows all of its subsidiary issues—race, family relationships, black psychology, social roles (particularly motherhood and womanhood), economic ethics—to rise to the surface. However, unlike the verisimilitude with which such issues arise in the Literature of Vivification, and for the black reader, in the Literature of Inversion, they appear here as ideology (which is, one should note, how a white reader would typically read a work of inversion), a fact made abundantly clear by the ideological response generated among *both* black *and* white readers. The result, as

Bakhtin's theory suggests, eliminates the dialogue between author and
reader (black or white); however dialectical it might be, the goals of
mythification, as with any body of philosophy, are a systematic,
monological body of thought (*Problems* 92–94).

Even more significant, however, in *Beloved*'s ascent as a paradigm of
mythification is the manner in which Morrison has overlaid the transparent
mythification rooted within the themes of the story itself with an
overarching metaphor of the process by which such myths are reified.
Beloved is the story of a woman who commits an act so bold and
outrageous, killing her baby to prevent the child from being taken into
slavery, that the action has no meaning at all apart from ideology. That
ideology—that slavery is so brutal that infanticide is not an inappropriate
response to it—does not make for effective myth, however. It is, in fact,
such a conspicuous rejection of traditional values that, were it not for the
ambivalent response in the book within the black community to the murder,
the novel would seem clearly to manifest the character of the Literature of
Inversion. However, it is not inversive. Otherwise, black readers would
read the work hypostatically, and that does not appear to have happened.

Morrison's purpose for the novel seems considerably more complex
than Sethe's misguided ideology. A reader's initial response, as the public
skirmish over the novel would demonstrate, is to either affirm or reject the
afrocentric awareness Morrison creates with such an unthinkable act and
the unambiguous ideology it posits, either by espousing a more holistic
African American myth—that slavery is so brutal it deprives its victims of
the opportunity to ever escape its emotional chains—or, in contrast,
attacking the novel's ideological excesses. The story, though, moves well
beyond the murder. Sethe has continued, for eighteen years, to live at the
home where the murder occurred, and after years of nightmarish
supernatural occurrences at 124, is confronted with the murdered baby's
corporeal ghost, returning in the body of a young woman, yet behaving and
talking like a baby. It is this appearance of the ghost itself, called
"Beloved," like the inscription from Sethe's baby's tombstone, which
undermines the more transparent inversive ideology and moves the book in
the direction of mythification. As Bakhtin reminds the critic, neither
monologism nor dialogism is a property of the text itself, but is instead a
result of the manner in which a text is contextualized (Hirschkop and

Shepherd 24–27). If history and memory and the evils of slavery were the point, Beloved need not appear at all.

The appearance of Beloved becomes the epicenter of the story, however, not because she becomes the source of conflict, driving the plot forward, but because she becomes the source of communication. Her arrival coincides with Paul D's, both recreating and frustrating Sethe's attempts to embrace the present. It is Beloved's appearance which opens Denver's past, and present, to her, much of it for the first time (61). Even so, it was Beloved's spectral presence which had destroyed earlier her opportunity to communicate at all (12–15). No one in the story, in fact, seems to be able to communicate apart from Beloved's presence—Sethe refuses to pass on her stories from Sweet Home to Denver, Denver plays alone and feels "worn out" by the loneliness, Paul D hides all of his personal history apart from the few fragments contained in his songs (61, 28–29, 39–42).

She is, strictly speaking, the "word" upon which the novel rests, and within whose signification resides the referent of the myth itself. And she serves that function not just for the novel, but for the story of the novel, and it is within the story of the novel that the myth she represents to Sethe, Paul D, even Denver, expands to include the myth of the novel itself. For Bakhtin, this shifting and unstable synthesis of what he calls "word" and "hero" in a novel is indicative of a work which cannot escape its monological nature; "a discourse truly adequate for the depiction of an ideological world," he writes, "can only be its own discourse" (*Speech Genres* 198).

What cannot be forgotten is that Beloved arrives at 124 with almost no language whatsoever. She is, at her essence (if a ghost can be said to possess an essence), Sethe's murdered baby; Sethe's overwhelming need to urinate at Beloved's arrival mirrors her water breaking at birth (51). But Beloved's need to consume cup after cup of water just as Sethe is voiding so much water suggests that Beloved exists as an extension of Sethe, or perhaps as a product of her, brought into existence as the reified manifestation of Sethe's unresolved grief. As such, she exists intricately intertwined with Sethe's emotions, a spatiotemporal representation of Sethe's words—an utterance, a signifier. Her references to and about Sethe reinforce that connection; she calls Sethe's mother "your woman," (61), suggesting that, for Beloved, Sethe exists as the central referent by which any object is named, which is precisely the case for the novel as well. Later, Beloved, almost trancelike, tells Denver of a face she sees in the darkness, apparently Sethe's, before announcing "It's me" (124). Much earlier, Beloved angrily confesses to Denver her substantive need for Sethe: "She is the one. She is the one I need. You can go but she is the one I have to have" (76).

So Beloved comes to 124 creating a language for Sethe—a language which begins to overflow almost immediately. At Beloved's prompting, Sethe tells deeply detailed stories about the "diamonds" Mrs. Garner had given her, about her mother's hanging (an event Denver had never, in eighteen years, heard recounted), about the births of unnumbered siblings which her mother just "threw away" because of their white fathers (58–63). Eventually, the reader is told, 124 becomes so loud, the noise can be heard from the road (169).

> What [Stamp Paid] heard, as he moved toward the porch, he didn't understand. Out on Bluestone Road he thought he heard a conflagration of hasty voices—loud, urgent, all speaking at once so he could not make out what they were talking about or to whom. The speech wasn't nonsensical, exactly, nor was it tongues. But something was wrong with the order of the words and he couldn't describe it or cipher it to save his life....he believed the undecipherable language clamoring around the house was the mumbling of the black and angry dead. (173, 198)

Beloved's ability to incite speech from the residents of 124 is made all the more obvious by the accounts they tell of previous incidents in which they (or loved ones) were unwilling, or unable, to speak. Halle could not respond to Sethe's rape at Sweet Home, nor could Paul D speak to Halle because of the iron bit in his mouth (69). Sethe cannot tell Denver about her rape and beating by schoolteacher and his nephews. At Sethe's arrival, Baby Suggs gives up preaching forever. Sethe and Baby Suggs together agree that the events of the past are unspeakable. Denver had even, at one point, gone deaf rather than confront Sethe's, and her own, past (104–05). Clearly, the language Beloved brings to 124 contains the essence of a family myth.

Ironically, the closer Sethe and the residents of 124 come to engaging in heteroglossic dialogue, shaping a meaning for each other which was not previously realized, the more vivid become their recollections of enslavement. That may be no coincidence; Bakhtin's concept of dialogue is, at its essence, strikingly similar to Friedrich Nietzsche's idea of the slave's servile, circumscribed, and reactive consciousness (Bernstein, "Poetics" 201). Michael Andre Bernstein, using language which sounds hauntingly Bakhtinian, notes that every thought the slave has and utters "is purely reactive, impregnated by the words and values of others and formulated entirely in response to and as an anticipation of the responses he will elicit" (201). At some point, the realization that dialogue creates an identical condition must have an effect on one who has been enslaved.

So perhaps the costs of slavery *are*, as Baby Suggs and Sethe agreed, literally unspeakable. Sethe herself, on the verge of leaving the legacy of the past behind—forgetting Halle, marrying Paul D, accepting Baby Suggs's spiritual message (metaphorically transformed into the phonetically similar "massage")—is struck down by a supernatural strangler, choked and bruised as if the "word" that Beloved represents had literally "stuck in her throat," just at the moment she seemed prepared to express it (96). She suspects Beloved, but can never verbalize it (97–99).

Furthermore, the legacy of schoolteacher riding up to 124 hangs over Sethe just as it hangs over the novel, and the reader finds, as Sethe does, the whole story of the baby's murder cycling around again and again whenever anything grows too promising. Just at the point where Paul D seems to have bridged the chasm of Sethe's guilt and grief by suggesting they have a baby (128–30), schoolteacher arrives again (metaphorically for Sethe, literally for the reader, in yet another manifestation of the story), one of the apocalyptic "four horsemen," and the entire episode is recounted in all its painful detail (148–53). It is clear that Sethe is afflicted with what Nietzsche calls *ressentiment*, an obsession borne of profound injury and the concomitant inability to either forget it or avenge it (Bernstein, "Poetics" 205). Bernstein seems to be describing Sethe when he indicates that the victim of *ressentiment* experiences "a maddening sense of impotence…united to a daemonically obsessive total recall, until the sufferer's entire consciousness is like an open sore whose sight evokes only disgust in both the victim…and those around [her]" (205). That condition becomes obvious when Sethe tries to explain her murder of the child to Paul D; the attempt fails when Paul D, echoing schoolteacher, compares Sethe to an animal (165). Even more painfully, the effect of the narrative, in spite of Sethe's assertions to the contrary, is as if she is trying to explain her actions to Beloved (159–65).

Sethe's response to the *ressentiment* is to move ever closer to Beloved. Eventually, she realizes who Beloved is, when Beloved hums a song only Sethe and her children could know (175–76). She comes to acknowledge the unity of identity she shares with Beloved, and gives up everything she has to placate Beloved's childlike, but hedonistic, desires. However, having a language through which to deal with guilt and grief does not create, for Sethe or the black reader, a shared myth; the more single-minded Sethe becomes in her attention to Beloved, the more alienated she becomes from everyone else.

The communication Beloved brings between Sethe and her family and community is destined to fail, because Beloved exists without a context, like a word uttered and simply hanging in space. Beloved's description of herself, most particularly the monologue near the end of the book (210–13), is often dense and disjointed, describing perhaps a grave, perhaps a womb, perhaps a hell, but in no case, any context through which might be opened anyone's understanding of a shared myth (either within the context of the novel, or among black readers). Actually, Beloved's existence may have meaning only when the reader, like Sethe, *believes* the myth *a priori* to understanding it, but such meaning is not formed through engagement, or dialogic, between Morrison and the reader, as "understanding" would entail, inasmuch as answerability is neither invited nor possible with *Beloved.* In fact, the only occasion in which a word uttered acontextually may be presumed to carry meaning is in the context of the sacred utterance; the word has meaning for all time precisely because it has no specific meaning for any specific time. If, as Nancy Peterson writes, criticism of Morrison's work is "unspeakable" ("Introduction" 162), then certainly a revisionary understanding of it, which would affirm the priority of the reader's response instead of the priority of the author's utterance, would be anathema (*Art and Answerability* 276–85).

As a result, Sethe's search for contextuality for Beloved results in the transference of materiality from Beloved herself to the product of Sethe's interpretation of Beloved, which, as is the case with any text, is always open to variant readings. For everyone but Sethe, Beloved's acontextual existence offers no greater understanding of Sethe, or her actions, or slavery; it only brings emotions of enmity. For Paul D, the feeling is guilt at having been seduced by her; for Denver, it is jealousy and selfishness; for the black residents in the community, it is fear. Conversely, contextualization may be privileged, according to Bakhtin, by intonation, or the verbal accents with which an utterance is delivered, which would not only stabilize iterability, but would secure the noncoincidence of the utterance with itself and its referent. However, Bakhtin points out that such a practice leaves no material traces, so that any intonation by which Beloved, as character, may have had meaning within the context of the community of 124 is indiscernible to the reader, and as such, is concealed by the intonation by which Beloved, the signifier, is presented to the reader ("Author and Hero" 104). When Sethe, Denver, and Beloved move into inner monologue, as they do for a significant period near the beginning of Part Two, their words are intoned as their own, concealed from the community around 124, but carry an intonation intended, apparently, to secure the reliability of their interpretation by the reader.

Inescapable in this analysis is the fact that, if Beloved is Sethe's utterance, she is also Morrison's utterance—both signifier and text. For this reason, Beloved might be considered to be Morrison's *sacred* utterance, offering no contextualized understanding for Sethe, who believes in Beloved and struggles on faith, and in vain, to make meaning of Beloved's existence, but providing a reader (especially a black reader, who must make the transformation from hypostatic reading to pragmatic reading in order for the text to move from ideology to myth) with an authoritative text in Beloved (and in *Beloved*) in which to stabilize a community, as any myth should accomplish. Three times in the novel's final two pages, Sethe (or Morrison) echoes the incantation that "This is not a story to pass on," and just as with Islamic prohibitions on the physical portrayal of Muhammad, Jesus Christ's insistence on the secrecy of his identity, and Jewish tradition regarding the unspeakability of the name of Yahweh, the effect is to intensify the myth and, inasmuch as "all that rises, converges," stabilize it. The presence of spirits only heightens the effect.

It is this fact which so clearly defines *Beloved* as an exemplar of the Literature of Mythification. Bakhtin and Buber are clear about the importance, in a dialogue, of the "Other," the presence of which makes the superaddressee (occupying the "between") the author's psychological arbiter of the text as creation-in-progress, or what may be called the author's inner speech. Every author is aware of the absolute "otherness" of the Other, African American authors of the otherness of two Others, and so she or he continually navigates around and through the superaddressee in an internal dialogue of creation, foregrounding for the author of mythification, not dialogue, but authority and legitimization. In fact, for Bakhtin, the utterances of one's inner speech are saturated with the evaluations of the superaddressee, and so the distance between author and reader is not only preserved as the author creates the work, but becomes a tool through which the author of a work of mythification can speak authoritatively. As a result, the struggle to convey a mythology to a perfectly understanding superaddressee produces a convergence of thought and internal dialogue which elevates the myth and produces what may be considered as the antithesis of consensus, or monologistic dissociation, with the reader. In fact, according to Bakhtin, the mere existence of theses and antitheses—that is, the existence of a dialectic—asserts an unresolvable monologicality. He writes, "Take a dialogue and remove the voices (the partitioning of voices), remove the intonations (emotional and individualizing ones), carve out abstract concepts and judgments from living words and responses, cram everything into one abstract consciousness—and that's how you get dialectics" (*Speech Genres* 147).

That *Beloved*, a crowning achievement of mythification, should come concurrent with Morrison's own literary beatification is no coincidence. Because a work of literary mythification posits "ideas, foreknowledge, and fancy" in such a manner as to create, not a portrayal of African American life, but a compelling and authoritative mythology about it, the assent of such a literature and its author to sacrosanctity would not be unexpected. Such is the origin of any sacred text. The evolution of critical opinion regarding Morrison's work, and Morrison herself, offers almost indisputable evidence of its place in the Literature of Mythification. Trudier Harris calls Morrison "a *phenomenon*,…a once-in-a-lifetime rarity, the literary equivalent of Paul Robeson, Michael Jordan, Wayne Gretzky, Chris Evert, or Martina Navratilova" (9). Nancy J. Peterson goes even further. In her essay "Introduction: Canonizing Toni Morrison," she exposes the near-sacred level to which Morrison has ascended by asserting how "unspeakable," "unimaginable," and "unthinkable" it would be to validate, or even mention, early criticism of Morrison's work (461–62).[2]

However, the making of a minion is never a reliable enterprise; even Michael Jordan (to use Trudier Harris's example) failed to make his junior high basketball team. The literary universe is even shakier than most. Morrison's first novel, *The Bluest Eye*, was rejected several times before Holt accepted it in 1970, and the book received fewer reviews even than Al Young's *Snakes*, another first novel by an African American writer, published the same season. Sales for her second novel, *Sula*, languished far below expectations and met with mixed critical opinion. Even after *Song of Solomon* won the National Book Critics Circle Award, it peaked on *Publisher's Weekly*'s bestseller list at number eleven, and disappeared from the list after a mere four weeks. At that point, in 1978, *Song of Solomon* had only 45,000 copies in print, compared with Colleen McCullough's *The Thorn Birds*, which in just three months had sold 590,287 copies (*Publishers Weekly* 34, 42).

Nevertheless, within a year of *The Bluest Eye*'s publication, *The New York Times* began calling on Morrison regularly to review books related to black life or by black authors. During one short span in 1971 and 1972, she wrote twenty-eight reviews for *The New York Times Book Review*, as well as an essay, "What the Black Woman Thinks about Women's Lib," for the *New York Times Magazine* (Blake 190). Not only did she become *the* spokesperson on race in New York, she kept her editorial position at Random House, where she continued to build a network of young protégés, which by this time had included Toni Cade Bambara, Gayl Jones, Claude Brown, Angela Davis, Henry Dumas, and Stokely Carmichael (McKay 2, Iannone 60).[3] She would tell an interviewer, with the prophetic confidence of a consummate mythifier, "I want to participate in developing a canon of Black work" (Samuels and Hudson-Weems ix).

Her subsequent novel, *Jazz*, continued her evolution toward an increasingly transparent mythification; her epigraph is from an earthen jar in gnostic Nag Hammadi, and the book's narrator claims to be a transcendent god with the power to influence reality (219–21). The result of such mythification is that, whatever it is about Toni Morrison that makes inconceivable any criticism of her work makes it equally inconceivable that she could ever write another novel. She did, of course; *Paradise*, published in 1997. Like her previous works, it was a complex intermingling of western and African myth, and, as is inevitable with the Literature of

Mythification and the monologism it posits, met with critical opinion which highlighted the book's monologistic traits—"heavy-handed, schematic writing," says one critic (Kakutani). He certainly meant the criticism to say that the language of the book renders it ineffectual, but for the Literature of Mythification, such a critique confirms the author's intent for the book, for as with any "sacred" text, authoritative discourse falls flat with those who reject such monologism.

For Morrison, however, mythification *is* the message. Her speech to the Nobel Committee in 1993 proposed the idea that "paradise" may be the province of language, and that such a journey is never easy. "Be it grand or slender," she tells her audience, "burrowing, blasting or refusing to sanctify; whether it laughs out loud or is a cry without an alphabet, the choice word or the chosen silence, unmolested language surges toward knowledge, not its destruction." She pushes forward:

> Word-work is sublime…because it is generative; it makes meaning that secures our difference, our human difference—the way in which we are like no other life.
> We die. That may be the meaning of life. But we *do* language. That may be the measure of our lives.

Conclusion

The Black "I" in the Twenty-First Century

A friend of Flannery O'Connor once offered to bring James Baldwin to
Andalusia for a visit. Baldwin had burst onto the literary scene about the
same time O'Connor had, in the early 1950s, and their commonality of
subject matter—religion and race—would have made a meeting between
the two of them a logical expectation. O'Connor, however, replied that
while she would visit with Baldwin in New York, she would not do so in
Milledgeville, saying, "I observe the traditions of the society I feed on—it's
only fair. Might as well expect a mule to fly as me to see James Baldwin in
Georgia" (Wood 109). Baldwin would scarcely have been the only black
man in Milledgeville, nor would anything that he had written to that point
make him the pariah O'Connor implied he would be. Instead, it was just the
prospect of *any* black man visiting Andalusia that would have scandalized
Milledgeville, and as bizarre as it may seem today, O'Connor likely knew
that too few of her neighbors would have considered Baldwin important
enough, if they knew who he was at all, to make him an exception to the
rules.

Fifty years have made a radical difference in the public's awareness of,
and respect for, African American writers. The prominence of African
American culture in the American mainstream over, especially, the past
twenty years or so has been remarkable; finding a contemporary college
student who has not, during his or her high school experience, read or
studied Baldwin, Hurston, Morrison, Langston Hughes, Terry McMillan,

or any number of other prominent black writers is almost impossible. African American Studies programs have sprung up at universities around the country, and black intellectuals have become almost as famous as the writers and politicians upon whom their careers are built, and in even more demand on university faculties. Colin Powell could have been president of the United States had he wanted to be. Toni Morrison won the Nobel Prize in Literature. One could persuasively argue that Michael Jordan is the most famous American ever to live. Popular African American art forms like rap music and break dancing have become the idiom of choice for an entire generation, and the fame enjoyed by Michael Jackson would dwarf that of William Faulkner, Ernest Hemingway, and F. Scott Fitzgerald combined. In light of these changes, to suggest that race will continue to be a black eye for the twenty-first century African American author would be outrageous, if not ridiculous.

At the same time, never has the diversity in black America been as pronounced as at the beginning of the twenty-first century. Family income rose faster for black America in 1999 than for any other racial or ethnic group, yet black poverty still continued to be one of America's major social problems. Black enrollment in universities continues at near record numbers, but still, more black men are in prison than in college. Black leaders crusade both for and against Affirmative Action. Conservative and Republican black men and women are becoming as prominent in government, business, and entertainment as those from the more liberal Democratic perspectives traditionally associated with black America. In other words, the black experience in the twenty-first century promises to birth writers who will live radically different lives from each other, and who will, as a result, bring a spectral dichotomy of emotions, passions, angers, ambitions, and skills to their work. As Flannery O'Connor reminds us, "The country that the writer is concerned with…is…the region that most immediately surrounds him" ("The Fiction Writer and His Country" 802). Furthermore, the most problematic of the black author's dual audiences, white America, has come to understand better its shared humanity with black America, which, when coupled with black America's changing economic and social status, creates the distinct likelihood that black writers will approach their dual audiences in the future with a different "superaddressee" than at present. For the foreseeable future,

African American authors will still be surrounded by matters of race, but the experience will almost certainly be even less homogeneous than it has been in the past.

This is one key reason African American literature continues to be so distinctive; it *does* reflect a diversity of styles and themes borne of the author's intentional balancing of a dual racial audience. The result, of course, will always be the sort of quaternary typology that my theory posits, but will need to allow, even more than my present theory does, for the possibility that the black author's dual audiences may move closer to each other in their reading of a work. To explore, as the book has done, how one renowned contemporary writer, such as Toni Morrison, communicates similar themes so differently from another, equally renowned, writer, such as August Wilson, or why a book like *High Cotton* seems so elusive in its theme will, I hope, play an important role in this generation's understanding of African American literature's rise to prominence during the twentieth century. What seems just as important, however, is helping the next generation of readers, black *and* white, and perhaps even the next generation of African American writers, understand how their changing social milieu, and changing attitudes about race, is changing African American novels, plays, and poems into something perhaps quite different from that of their literary predecessors.

In practical terms, for a contemporary critic to continue suggesting that African American literature speaks too directly to the "African" experience and not as much to the "American" experience, as was frequently said during the twentieth century, seems today to be anachronistic—the black experience in America is more likely than ever to share an emotional framework with whites. In truth, black literature may have always been more American than white literature, given the latter's traditional use of European forms and need for European approval (Gates, *Loose Canons* 22–29). By the same token, to expect African American literary works to convey a kind of racial narcissism is to place an overemphasis on shared characteristics and experiences between a narrative and its reader, an expectation which seems so overflowing with identity politics that only the most factional, and naive, of literary traditions would embrace it (although works written from such a perspective do show up among the Literature of Inversion). Certainly, for as far as anyone can see into the twenty-first century, double-conscious black writers will be forced to continue balancing the racial expectations of a dual audience as they create their works. What remains to be seen, however, is whether generations coming of age in the twenty-first century will notice.

That is one reason books like this exist. Literary traditions share much in common with social rituals and institutions; they exist because they once justified the reality of a certain worldview. Sociologist Peter Berger calls them, for that reason, "plausibility structures." The foundation upon which such plausibility structures exist, Berger writes, is a web of "legitimation," the process by which the social world is explained and justified to a society's members (Berger and Luckmann, *Social Construction* 58). That web of legitimation grows in importance with each subsequent generation, for while the first generation may know intimately the rationale for the existence of an institution or tradition, the second generation will know only the institution or tradition itself, distanced as they are from the circumstances that inspired its creation. Subsequent generations may find the tradition completely unnecessary for the purposes for which it was created, but by that time, its purposes have become communal, reality-maintaining, and are thus essential to the society for no reason other than their capacity to hold the society together. Because the tradition no longer serves any discernable pragmatic purpose, however, it must be justified and explained to all new members of the society within each subsequent generation, or, as Berger puts it, "firmly anchored in subjective certainty," in order to continue to serve its purpose (*Rumor* 53). In other words, it must be "legitimated."

To survive as a distinct literary tradition for another hundred years, African American literature may need to be legitimated to future generations. Theories of difference, such as the typology in this book, are precisely the sort of explanation of a phenomenon (i.e., legitimation) upon which plausibility structures are built. The black literary tradition *is* different, and critics will continue to debate why for years to come. Some explanations will become irrelevant with the changing times, and this theory may well be one of them. For the present, however, these theories serve to inspire subsequent generations with a sense of the price paid by the African American literary tradition to become what it has become, and the importance of preserving that difference into the future. A critic's hope, in spite of the cryptic and obfuscating language we use, is that converts will come to love the literature as much as we do, and will work, as this book has done, to understand the tradition better.

This was part of my own experience even in the writing of this book. One of my early attractions to African American literature was its virtuosity in handling magical, supernatural (even spiritual) issues, so among my first literary passions were the stories of Henry Dumas. I had been introduced to Dumas's work in 1990 by the African American writer John McClusky, and within a year I had enrolled in my first African American Literature class. The fact that Dumas had worked for economic justice in the 1960s and had been murdered by a policeman in a New York subway station only heightened the veneration I had for him and his literary efforts. By 1995, though, after four years of graduate classes and the rereading of his corpus in preparation for this book, I came to realize just how seriously flawed Dumas's fiction was. (His poems are less so.) I almost jettisoned my plans to include him in this book, but decided, probably for no better reason than nostalgia, to continue with the analysis of his fiction as an exemplar of the Literature of Inversion. Somewhere on the journey, I came to understand Dumas's authorial goals in a way I hadn't before, and in the process, became more willing not just to excuse, but to appreciate, his decisions to use obscure symbolism or to create cardboard characters who single-mindedly chase his themes. I ultimately understood the Literature of Inversion better by seeing Dumas's efforts at making his work inversive.

After five years, this typology has become the lens through which I now read all African American literature. I have particularly enjoyed the clever subversion in many of Charles Chesnutt's stories, but I could not overlook the mythification when I read Octavia Butler's *Kindred*, or the vivification when I read Ernest Gaines's *A Lesson Before Dying*, or the inversion in Charles Johnson's *Middle Passage*. My efforts in formulating this theory have been guided by the principle that African American literature should be judged by the same standards that other art is judged: its ability to capture the soul of a votary and speak to the experience common to all of us—life and death, pain and celebration, hope and despair…the human experience. African American literature has many ways of doing that.

What a typology like the one in this work ought to do, then, for future readers of African American literature is just what it did for me—elevate the appreciation of African American literature by demystifying its methods. In the process, the clearer vision that the reader gains of "the black 'I'" who composed the work reduces the possibility that the author...and the work...will have to bear the social consequences that have always accompanied the black eye of race.

Notes

Introduction: The African American Writer's Dilemma

[1] See Dorothy J. Hale's book, *Social Formalism: The Novel in Theory from Henry James to the Present* (especially pp. 202–08), for an excellent discussion regarding the ambiguity in Du Bois's various explanations of "double-consciousness," as well as her position that theorists have erroneously conflated the concepts of "double-consciousness" and "double-voicing."

[2] James Boswell records Samuel Johnson saying that "A woman's preaching is like a dog's walking on his hind legs. It is not done well, but you are surprised to find it done at all" (July 31, 1763). This attitude seems to be at the root of testimonials proffered in the front matter of early African American texts attesting their authenticity, such as the letter from John Wheatley in *Poems on Various Subjects, Religious and Moral* (1773), by Phillis Wheatley, or the letter from Edmund Quincy and the preface written by J. C. Hathaway at the front of *Narrative of William Wells Brown, A Fugitive Slave* (1847), by William Wells Brown.

[3] *The Conjure Woman* (1889), by Charles Chesnutt, *The Souls of Black Folk* (1903), by W.E.B. Du Bois, and *The Autobiography of an Ex-Coloured Man* (1912), by James Weldon Johnson, were among books by Negro writers that had a significant impact on the first decade of the twentieth century; in 1917, Claude McKay published three of his poems in

Seven Arts, a white journal; also in 1917, three plays with black casts opened on Broadway, the first time such a black presence had been seen on the Broadway stage; the Niagara Movement (1905) refocused the black agenda, and its progeny, the NAACP, galvanized Negro unity, even in the artistic realm (see Thomas R. Cripps, "The Reaction of the Negro to the Motion Picture *Birth of a Nation*," *The Historian* 25 (1963): 344–62). David Levering Lewis has called this attempt to alter social conditions through the arts "civil rights by copyright" (*W. E. B. Du Bois: The Fight for Equality* 153–82).

[4]Certainly an authenticating introduction offers no proof at all of the black writer's literary intentions with respect to the audience, but at least one such work, Henry Bibb's *Narrative of the Life and Adventures of Henry Bibb, an American Slave* (1850), offers a separate "Author's Preface" which reinforces the author's intent to place his/her work into "the public ear."

[5]Not at all typical, but perhaps consummately representative, of such enthusiasm was Carl Van Vechten, a wealthy New York socialite whose interest in the Harlem Renaissance and the promotion of the emerging black writers was remarkable, and in some ways assured the Harlem Renaissance's crossover appeal. Among his protégés and sincere friends were James Weldon Johnson, Langston Hughes, Chester Himes, Nella Larson, and Zora Neale Hurston (as well as such white artists as F. Scott Fitzgerald, George Gershwin, Laurence Olivier, and Thomas Mann). He carried on lifelong friendships with these writers and vigorously promoted newcomers, telling Hughes late in his life, "you and I have been through so many new Negroes that we are a little tired of it" (Kellner 290). It was Van Vechten that Hurston leaned on for support through the crisis of her false arrest in 1948, writing in a remarkably candid letter to him that: "I care nothing for anything anymore....My race has seen fit to destroy me without reason, and with the vilest tools conceived of by man so far....All that I have ever tried to do has proved useless. All that I have ever believed in has failed me. I have resolved to die" (Howard 144). Such venomous race-centered criticism was a circumstance with which Van Vechten would have been familiar, and by which he was equally surprised. His 1914 novel *Nigger Heaven*, conceived out of a belief that Harlem culture was so rich that it paled any other in America and that an objective portrayal of it was

the only way to capture its passion, was met with considerable disdain from the black community he had tried so honestly (and affectionately) to portray. His friends—Johnson, Hughes, Alice Dunbar Nelson—were impressed by the work, and publicly dismissed the controversy as a response to the title by reviewers who had not bothered even to read it. Johnson clearly conveys his support for Van Vechten, as well as a backhanded slap at the broader white literary establishment, when he writes, "The author pays colored people the rare tribute of writing about them as people rather than puppets" (Leuders 88).

[6]Though perhaps the rawest look at black culture might have been Van Vechten's novel (see note 4), the writers mentioned came under heavy criticism, especially from Du Bois, for their stark social realism in their portrayals of black urban life (Stepto 122).

[7]According to Houston Baker in "Generational Shifts and the Recent Criticism of Afro-American Literature," two philosophical waves are responsible for this position—the Black Aesthetic, promoted in the 1960s as an alternative to a perceived single, white-biased standard for evaluating literature; and a race-sensitive Marxian paradigm, posited by Baker himself, Henry Louis Gates, and Robert Stepto, among others, that rejects the "uncritical imposition upon Afro-American culture of literary theories borrowed from prominent white scholars" (12).

[8]Other notable works that use some variation of this approach would include Houston A. Baker, Jr.'s *Blues, Ideology, and Afro-American Literature* (1984), Robert B. Stepto's *From Behind the Veil* (1991), and Gayl Jones's *Liberating Voices* (1992). Toni Morrison's *Playing in the Dark* (1992) might be considered to represent a more tempered contemporary version of the second approach.

[9]Buber's work is significantly more nuanced and complex than my use of it suggests. My work will not intentionally misrepresent Buber or his dialogical ideas, but on the other hand, my purpose is not a Buberian analysis of African American literature. Buber's work is a foundation for my own analysis. Also, Buber's terms, "Ich–Du" and "Ich–Es," may possess subtle shades of meaning in the original language which are not explored in this work, but the terms are best known in English as "I–Thou" and "I–It," and so those more common English translations will be used in this work.

1. The Author/Audience Dialogue as Theoretical Perspective

[1]Amiri Baraka writes in "The Myth of a 'Negro Literature,'" that "a literature written in imitation of the meanest of social intelligences to be found in American culture, i.e., the white middle class..., even if its 'characters' *are* black, takes on the emotional barrenness of its model" (110).

[2]Bakhtin is clear in his assertion that the author reaches forward as he or she writes, composing with his or her audience's (or for a black author, audiences') potential response(s) clearly in mind, and that those expectations shape the final work. Bakhtin writes, "from the very beginning, the utterance is constructed while taking into account possible responsive reactions, for whose sake, in essence, it is actually created" (*Speech Genres* 94).

[3]This project, unifying art and life in literary production, seems to be an early attempt by Bakhtin to challenge the formalists, and to distance himself from their philosophical pursuits. The work cited in the text, "Art and Answerability," appears to have been written in response to Victor Shklovsky's famous essay "Art as Technique" (1917).

[4]In spite of the sardonic political tone of West's categories, some of his disdain for these strategies is aesthetic. To those who would pursue the "Booker T. Temptation," he states that the most creative and profound black writers will usually remain merely marginal to the mainstream, who, he suggests, are prone to celebrate black "flashes in the pan to satisfy faddish tokenism" (26). Those who succeed, he says, will inevitably lose their creativity. To those who would choose to "Go It Alone," he cautions that intellectual growth, development, and maturity is impossible without an engagement with a creative community (27). Nevertheless, at least a portion of his disdain seems social—defining as "arrogant" the attempt to become a participant in the "talented tenth," W. E. B. Du Bois's term for the cream of black intellectual and social achievers, or connecting someone's efforts to Booker T. Washington, which, throughout the twentieth century, has been akin to connecting them to Uncle Tom. In other words, some of West's terminology seems chosen merely to insult.

[5]This typology is, strictly speaking, a typology of literary types, not a typology of African American authors. Nevertheless, my own conclusions

about the typology, given its construction through authorial position and psychological approach to a dual audience, as inferred through an assumed superaddressee, is that in most cases an author's total body of work would likely wind up in one category. Only extenuating circumstances, such as the diversity of literary skills and social circumstances of Zora Neale Hurston, or a significant change in a writer's beliefs, would seem to provide a reason for a writer's work to reflect a different "literary type." In other words, this would not appear to be something that a writer would consciously choose for a work; the author's choice, and an unconscious one at that, would be to "please" the superaddressee, to be secure in one's accord with his or her dual audience. That, it would seem, would reflect an author's type as much as a book's.

3. The Literature of Subversion

[1]This fact is never specified in the novel, but is easily deduced by comparing the details of her appearance in the novel with details documented in biographical sources, particularly Hank O'Neal's work.

4. The Literature of Vivification

[1]Though I use both the masculine and feminine pronouns, most recorded slave narratives were authored by men, and narratives of the time written by women—stories such as Harriet Jacobs's *Incidents in the Life of a Slave Girl* (1861) or Harriet E. Wilson's novel, *Our Nig* (1853)—offer ample reason to believe that the female slave narrative may have assumed different forms from those written by men. Consider Berniece's plea to Boy Willie that he consider not just his forefathers' roles, but also his foremothers', in the family slave narrative: "Money can't buy what that piano cost. You can't sell your soul for money....Mama Ola polished this piano with her tears for seventeen years. She rubbed on it till her hands bled. Then she rubbed the blood in…mixed up with the rest of the blood on it. You always talking about your daddy, but you ain't looked to see what this foolishness cost your mother" (50–52).

[2]In the integrated phase of the slave narrative, such as that manifested by Berniece and Doaker, any icon would always remain unused, and even

above the possibility of use, having acquired what sociologist Emile Durkheim called "sacred" status (52–57). According to Durkheim, the value of a sacred object lies in its ability to achieve results beyond its mere pragmatic utility—results such as beckoning the presence of spirits or offering physical protection—and as a result, would be compromised by putting it to practical use. Such use would place the object within the realm of the everyday, or what Durkheim called the "profane." That Berniece finally decides to play the piano in the climactic scene should be interpreted in light of the fact that her use for it is totally sacred (that is, as a relic by which to solicit the aid of spiritual ancestors in the family's present conflict with Sutter's spirit, and not as a mere musical instrument), and therefore represents no change at all in her position regarding the piano and its value.

5. The Literature of Mythification

[1]Gina Wisker suggests that the accusation that Morrison and other black woman writers seem so provincial has a feminist rationale—that their viewpoint rejects making the black woman and the black woman's text the "male object of gaze." Inasmuch as most readers, male or female, have learned to read from the "gazing male" perspective, anything else seems to lack "universality" ("Introduction" 15). The result is that "art" comes to be defined by that singular standard, which has for most of American history been refined by white male critics, teachers, and so forth. Creative works that fail to meet that standard not only lack "universality," but are assumed to carry an explicit message, to constitute what might be called "propaganda."

[2]The mythification of Morrison herself is perhaps best exemplified by the evolution of her physical portrayal. The book-size photo of Morrison on the dustjacket of *The Bluest Eye* seems designed to convey a young black radical. By *Sula*, just three years later, the full-cover facial shot of the young radical has yielded to a small portrait, half darkened by shadows, on the inside backflap of the dustjacket. Though she still wears what would have been called an "afro" hairstyle, she appears fifteen years older and looks more like a suburban neighbor or office coworker than an urban radical.

Newsweek featured Morrison on its March 30, 1981, cover, following the publication of *Tar Baby*, making her the first black woman since Zora Neale Hurston in 1943 to appear on the cover of a national magazine (Peterson 463). Her response to the proposal was to quip, "Are you really going to put a middle-aged, gray haired colored lady on the cover of this magazine?" (Strouse 52). She was, indeed, becoming a more mature literary product—the dustjacket photos on *Song of Solomon* and *Tar Baby* highlighted Morrison's next-door-neighbor qualities, smile more relaxed, hair less tightly curled. *Beloved* used, for the first time since Morrison left Holt, the full back cover for a tight facial shot. It was the culmination of what had been occurring since her move to Knopf—an increasing intimacy and maturity with each new novel—and it serves as an evolutionary mirror-image of the photo on *The Bluest Eye*, revealing the gradual emergence of a wiser, gentler Toni Morrison.

The photo on the cover of *Jazz*, her first novel after *Beloved* and her first since receiving the Nobel Prize, is even more remarkable. Her head framed in a halo of light, Morrison no longer looks at the reader, but gazes knowingly into the distance. Her face is only partially illuminated, but what light there is causes her skin to glow and reveals enough of her advanced age to evoke the idea of a sage or even a goddess. Her hair appears, between *Beloved* and *Jazz*, to have been transformed into some new consistency, and appears as though it is powdered. It is a remarkable photo considered by itself, but as the culmination of the series of images she has presented to the public over the years, it stands in sharp contrast to the "merely mortal" author of her early days.

The same powerful effect is reproduced on the dustjacket of *Playing in the Dark*, her book of essays on race and literature published in 1992. On both front and back, she stands full-body, dimly lit, gazing into the distance. A sliver of light, like an eclipse or a crescent moon, or some undefined cosmic event, is all that accompanies her. She wears a wide belt, a string of pearls, and a cloth coat, fashionable at the time but reminiscent of the 1950s. She carries a wide-brimmed straw hat, evocative of those that may have been worn in the cotton fields early in the twentieth century. The entire look is like a specter from the past, but the effect is one of reverence and awe, not nostalgia. It is the beatified Toni Morrison, revealed, with no ambiguity, as an icon uniquely deserving of the Nobel Prize.

[3]Claude Brown, author of the acclaimed *Manchild in the Promised*

Land (1965), whose manuscript Morrison read during its creation, and Stokely Carmichael were Morrison's students at Howard University. They did not publish with Random House. Henry Dumas, by this time, was dead, having been murdered by a policeman in New York; his work, however, was influential on a generation of black writers, including Morrison.

Works Cited

Andrews, William. "The Representation of Slavery and the Rise of Afro-American Literary Realism, 1865–1920." In McDowell and Rampersad, *Slavery and the Literary Imagination* 62–80.

Anyidoho, Kofi. "Language and Development Strategy in Pan-African Literary Experience." *Research in African Literatures* 23.1 (1992): 45–63.

Atlas, Marilyn Judith. "Toni Morrison's *Beloved* and the Reviewers." *Midwestern Miscellany* 18 (1990): 45–57.

Awkward, Michael. *Inspiring Influences: Tradition, Revision, and Afro-American Women's Novels*. New York: Columbia University Press, 1989.

Baker, Houston, Jr. *Blues, Ideology, and Afro-American Literature: A Vernacular Theory*. Chicago: University of Chicago Press, 1984.

———. "Generational Shifts and the Recent Criticism of Afro-American Literature." *Black American Literature Forum* 23.2 (1981): 3–21.

Bakhtin, M. M. *Art and Answerability: Early Philosophical Essays*. Eds. Michael Holquist and Vadim Liapunov. Tr. Vadim Liapunov. Austin: University of Texas Press, 1990.

———. "Author and Hero in Aesthetic Activity." In *Art and Answerability: Early Philosophical Essays* 4–256.

———. *The Dialogic Imagination: Four Essays*. Ed. Michael Holquist. Tr. Caryl Emerson. Austin: University of Texas Press, 1981.

————. "Discourse in the Novel." In *The Dialogic Imagination: Four Essays* 259–422.

————. *Problems of Dostoevsky's Poetics.* Tr. Caryl Emerson. Minneapolis: University of Minnesota Press, 1984.

————. *Rabelais and His World.* Tr. Hélène Iswolsky. Cambridge, MA: MIT, 1968.

————. *Speech Genres and Other Late Essays.* Eds. Caryl Emerson and Michael Holquist. Tr. Vern W. McGee. Austin: University of Texas Press, 1986.

Baraka, Amiri. *Home, Social Essays.* New York: William Morrow, 1966.

————. "The Myth of a Negro Literature." In *Home, Social Essays* 105–15.

Baraka, Amiri, and Larry Neal, eds. *Black Fire: An Anthology of Afro-American Writing.* New York: William Morrow, 1968.

Barnes, Djuna. *Nightwood.* 1937. New York: New Directions, 1961.

Bell, Bernard W. *The Afro-American Novel and Its Tradition.* Amherst: University of Massachusetts Press, 1987.

Bell, Janet Cheatham. *Famous Black Quotations.* New York: Warner, 1995.

Benston, Kimberly W. *Speaking for You: The Vision of Ralph Ellison.* Washington, DC: Howard University Press, 1987.

Berenson, Bernard. "Value." *Aesthetics and History in the Visual Arts.* New York: Pantheon, 1948. Rpt. in *The Horizon Reader.* Ed. Harry Brent and William Lutz. New York: St. Martin's, 1992: 790–98.

Berger, Peter L. *A Rumor of Angels.* Garden City, NY: Doubleday, 1969.

Berger, Peter L., and Thomas Luckmann. *The Social Construction of Reality.* Garden City, NY: Doubleday, 1966.

Bernstein, Michael André. *Bitter Carnival:* Ressentiment *and the Abject Hero.* Princeton: Princeton University Press, 1992.

————. "The Poetics of *Ressentiment.*" In Morson and Emerson, *Rethinking Bakhtin: Extensions and Challenges* 197–224.

Bibb, Henry. *Narrative of the Life and Adventures of Henry Bibb, An American Slave.* 1850. New York: Negro University Press, 1969.

Blackburn, Sara. "You Still Can't Go Home Again." *New York Times Book Review* 30 Dec. 1973: 3.

Blake, Susan L. "Toni Morrison." In Davis and Harris, *Dictionary of*

Literary Biography, Volume 33 187–98.

Bond, Cynthia. "Language, Speech, and Difference in *Their Eyes Were Watching God.*" In Gates and Appiah, *Zora Neale Hurston: Critical Perspectives Past and Present* 204–17.

Boswell, James. *The Life of Samuel Johnson, LL.D.* New York: Everyman's Library, 1811.

Brown, Claude. *Manchild in the Promised Land.* New York: Macmillan, 1965.

Brown, Sterling, Arthur P. Davis, and Ulysses Lee. *The Negro Caravan.* New York: Dryden, 1941.

Brown, William Wells. *Narrative of William Wells Brown, A Fugitive Slave.* 1847. Reading, MA: Addison-Wesley, 1969.

Buber, Martin. *Between Man and Man.* London: Kegan Paul, 1947.

———. *I and Thou.* Tr. Ronald Gregor Smith. 1923. New York: Scribners, 1959.

Byerman, Keith E. *Fingering the Jagged Grain: Tradition and Form in Recent Black Fiction.* Athens: University of Georgia Press, 1985.

Carter, Steven. *Reflections of an Affirmative Action Baby.* New York: Basic, 1992.

Chatman, Seymour. *Story and Discourse: Narrative Structure in Fiction and Film.* Ithaca: Cornell University Press, 1978.

Chesnutt, Charles. *The Conjure Woman and Other Tales.* 1889. Ann Arbor: University of Michigan Press, 1983.

Cripps, Thomas R. "The Reaction of the Negro to the Motion Picture *Birth of a Nation.*" *The Historian* 25 (1963): 344–62.

Crouch, Stanley. "Aunt Media." *New Republic* 19 Oct. 1987: 38–43.

Davis, Thadious, and Trudier Harris, eds. *Dictionary of Literary Biography, Volume 33.* Detroit: Gale, 1987.

De Beauvoir, Simone. *The Second Sex.* New York: Knopf, 1952.

De Man, Paul. "Dialogue and Dialogism." In Morson and Emerson, *Rethinking Bakhtin: Extensions and Challenges* 105–14.

———. *The Resistance to Theory.* Minneapolis: University of Minnesota Press, 1986.

DeVore, Lynn. "The Backgrounds of *Nightwood*: Robin, Felix, and Nora." *Journal of Modern Literature* 10.1 (1983): 71–90.

Dixon, Melvin. *Ride Out the Wilderness: Geography and Identity in Afro-*

American Literature. Urbana: University of Illinois Press, 1987.

Du Bois, W. E. B. *The Souls of Black Folk*. 1903. New York: Dodd, Mead, 1961.

Dumas, Henry. *Ark of Bones, and Other Stories*. Ed. Hale Chatfield and Eugene Redmond. Carbondale: Southern Illinois University Press, 1970.

Durkheim, Emile. *The Elementary Forms of the Religious Life*. 1912. New York: Free Press, 1965.

Eder, Richard. *Los Angeles Times Book Review* 23 Feb. 1992: 3.

Elkins, Marilyn, ed. *August Wilson: A Casebook*. New York: Garland, 1994.

Ellison, Ralph. *Invisible Man*. New York: Random House, 1952.

———. *Shadow and Act*. New York: Random House, 1953.

Fein, Esther B. "A Writer, but Not a Black Everyman." *New York Times* 9 Apr. 1992: C: 17.

Fichte, Johann. *The Vocation of Man*. 1800. Indianapolis: Hackett, 1987.

Fleche, Anne. "The History Lesson: Authenticity and Anachronism in August Wilson's Plays." In Nadel, *May All Your Fences Have Gates: Essays on the Drama of August Wilson* 9–20.

Frank, Joseph. *The Widening Gyre*. New Brunswick, NJ: Rutgers University Press, 1963.

Franklin, John Hope. "History of Racial Segregation in the United States." In Meier and Rudwick, *The Black Community in Modern America* 3–20.

Frann, Michael. "Displacing Castration: *Nightwood, Ladies Almanack*, and Feminine Writing." *Contemporary Literature* 30.1 (1989): 33–58.

Frost, Robert. *Mountain Interval*. New York: Henry Holt, 1916.

Furman, Jan. *Toni Morrison's Fiction*. Columbia: University of South Carolina Press, 1996.

Gaines, Ernest. *A Lesson Before Dying*. New York: Knopf, 1993.

Gantt, Patricia. "Ghosts from 'Down There': The Southernness of August Wilson." In Elkins, *August Wilson: A Casebook* 69–88.

Gates, Henry Louis, Jr. "The Great Black Hope." *Washington Post Book World* 23 Feb. 1992: 1.

———. *Loose Canons*. New York: Oxford University Press, 1992.

———. *The Signifying Monkey; A Theory of African-American Literary*

Criticism. New York: Oxford University Press, 1988.

————. "'What's Love Got to Do with It?': Critical Theory, Integrity, and the Black Idiom." *New Literary History* 18.2 (1987): 345–62.

Gates, Henry Louis, Jr., ed. *"Race," Writing, and Difference.* Chicago: University of Chicago Press, 1985.

Gates, Henry Louis, Jr., and Anthony Appiah, eds. *Zora Neale Hurston: Critical Perspectives Past and Present.* New York: Amistad, 1993.

Gayle, Addison, ed. *The Black Aesthetic.* New York: Doubleday, 1971.

Gilbert, Herman Cromwell. "Henry Dumas and the Flood of Life." *Black American Literature Forum* 22.2 (1988): 238–40.

Greiner, Donald J. "Antony Lamont in Search of Gilbert Sorrentino: Character and *Mulligan Stew.*" *Review of Contemporary Fiction* 1.1 (1981): 104–12.

Hale, Dorothy J. *Social Formalism: The Novel in Theory from Henry James to the Present.* Stanford: Stanford University Press, 1998.

Haley, Alex. *Roots.* New York: Delta, 1976.

Harris, Trudier. "Toni Morrison: Solo Flight Through Literature into History." *World Literature Today* 68 (1994): 9–14.

Harris, Trudier, and Thadious Davis, eds. *Dictionary of Literary Biography, Volume 51.* Detroit: Gale, 1987.

Hathaway, J. C. Preface. *Narrative of William Wells Brown, A Fugitive Slave.* By William Wells Brown. 1847. Reading, MA: Addison-Wesley, 1969.

Hegel, G. W. F. *The Philosophy of History.* 1832. Buffalo: Prometheus, 1990.

Henderson, Stephen. *Understanding the New Black Poetry, Black Speech and Black Music as Poetic References.* New York: William Morrow, 1973.

Herrmann, Anne. *The Dialogic and Difference: "An/other Woman" in Virginia Woolf and Christa Wolf.* New York: Columbia University Press, 1987.

Hirschkop, Ken, and David Shepherd. *Bakhtin and Cultural Theory.* New York: St. Martin's, 1989.

Howard, Lillie P. "Zora Neale Hurston." In Harris and Davis, *Dictionary of Literary Biography, Volume 51* 133-145.

Hurston, Zora Neale. *Dust Tracks on a Road.* 1942. New York: Harper,

1991.

———. "How It Feels to Be Colored Me." *World Tomorrow* 11 (May 1928): 215–16.

———. *Their Eyes Were Watching God*. 1937. Urbana: University of Illinois Press, 1991.

———. "What White Publishers Won't Print." *Negro Digest* 8 (Apr. 1950): 85–89.

Iannone, Carol. "Toni Morrison's Career." *Commentary* 84.6 (Dec. 1987): 59–63.

Jacobs, Harriet. *Incidents in the Life of a Slave Girl*. 1861. New York: Oxford University Press, 1988.

Johnson, Barbara. "Thresholds of Difference: Structures of Address in Zora Neale Hurston." In Gates, *"Race," Writing, and Difference* 317–28.

Johnson, Charles. *Middle Passage*. New York: Atheneum, 1990.

Johnson, James Weldon. *The Autobiography of an Ex-Coloured Man*. 1912. New York: Penguin, 1990.

Jones, Gayl. *Liberating Voices: Oral Tradition in African American Literature*. New York: Penguin, 1992.

Jones, LeRoi, and Larry Neal, eds. *Black Fire: An Anthology of Afro-American Writing*. New York: William Morrow, 1968.

Jones, Malcolm V. *Dostoyevsky After Bakhtin: Readings in Dostoyevsky's Fantastic Realism*. Cambridge: Cambridge University Press, 1990.

Jordan, Elaine. "'Not My People': Toni Morrison and Identity." In Wisker, *Black Women's Writing* 108–22.

Joyce, Joyce A. "The Black Canon: Reconstructing Black American Literary Criticism." *New Literary History* 18.2 (1987): 335–44.

Kakutani, Michiko. "Worthy Women, Unredeemable Men." *The New York Times* 6 Jan. 1998, D: 1.

Kannenstine, Louis F. *The Art of Djuna Barnes: Duality and Damnation*. New York: New York University Press, 1977.

Kelley, William Melvin. *Dunsfords Travels Everywheres*. New York: Doubleday, 1970.

Kellner, Bruce. *Carl Van Vechten and the Irreverent Decades*. Norman: University of Oklahoma Press, 1968.

Kennedy, Randall. *Race, Crime, and the Law*. New York: Pantheon, 1997.

Klotman, Phyllis Rauch. *Another Man Gone: The Black Runner in Contemporary Afro-American Literature.* Port Washington, NY: Kennikat, 1977.

Leuders, Edward. *Carl Van Vechten and the Twenties.* Albuquerque: University of New Mexico Press, 1955.

Lewis, David Levering. *W. E. B. Du Bois, Biography of a Race: 1868–1919.* New York: Holt, 1994.

———. *W. E. B. Du Bois, The Fight for Equality and the American Century: 1919–1963.* New York: Holt, 2000.

Locke, Alain. *The New Negro.* 1925. New York: Scribner, 1997.

Marshall, Paule. *Praisesong for the Widow.* New York: Putnam, 1983.

Marvin, P. H. "The Bluest Eye." *Library Journal* 95 (Nov. 1, 1970): 3806.

McDowell, Deborah E., and Arnold Rampersad, eds. *Slavery and the Literary Imagination.* Baltimore: Johns Hopkins University Press, 1989.

McKay, Nellie Y., ed. *Critical Essays on Toni Morrison.* Boston: G.K. Hall, 1988.

———. "Introduction." In McKay, *Critical Essays on Toni Morrison* 1–18.

McKnight, Reginald. *I Get on the Bus.* Boston: Little, Brown, 1990.

Medvedev, Pavel. *The Formal Method in Literary Scholarship: A Critical View.* Tr. Albert Wehrle. Cambridge: Harvard University Press, 1985.

Meier, August, and Elliott Rudwick, eds. *The Black Community in Modern America.* Vol. 2 of *The Making of Black America.* 2 vols. New York: Atheneum, 1969.

Miller, James. "Bigger Thomas's Quest for Voice and Audience in Richard Wright's *Native Son.*" *Callaloo* 9 (1986): 501–06.

Monaco, Pamela Jean. "Father, Son, and Holy Ghost: From the Local to the Mythical in August Wilson." In Elkins, *August Wilson: A Casebook* 89–104.

Morales, Michael. "Ghosts on the Piano: August Wilson and the Representation of Black American History." In Nadel, *May All Your Fences Have Gates: Essays on the Drama of August Wilson* 105–15.

Morrison, Toni. *Beloved.* New York: Knopf, 1987.

———. *The Bluest Eye.* New York: Holt, 1970.

————. *Jazz*. New York: Knopf, 1992.

————. *Paradise*. New York: Knopf, 1998.

————. *Playing in the Dark: Whiteness and the Literary Imagination*. Cambridge: Harvard University Press, 1992.

————. *Song of Solomon*. New York: Knopf, 1977.

————. *Sula*. New York: Knopf, 1973.

————. *Tar Baby*. New York: Knopf, 1981.

————. "Unspeakable Things Unspoken: The Afro-American Presence in American Literature." *Michigan Quarterly Review* 28.1 (Winter 1989): 9–34.

Morson, Gary Saul, and Caryl Emerson. *Mikhail Bakhtin: Creation of a Prosaics*. Stanford: Stanford University Press, 1990.

————. *Rethinking Bakhtin: Extensions and Challenges*. Evanston, IL: Northwestern University Press, 1989.

Nadel, Alan, ed. *May All Your Fences Have Gates: Essays on the Drama of August Wilson*. Iowa City: University of Iowa Press, 1994.

Natoli, Joseph. "Tracing a Beginning Through Past Theory Voices." In Natoli, *Tracing Literary Theory* 3–26.

Natoli, Joseph, ed. *Tracing Literary Theory*. Urbana: University of Illinois Press, 1987.

Neal, Larry. "And Shine Swam On." In Jones and Neal, *Black Fire: An Anthology of Afro-American Writing* 638–56.

————. "Ellison's Zoot Suit." In Benston, *Speaking for You: The Vision of Ralph Ellison* 105–24.

O'Connor, Flannery. "The Fiction Writer and His Country." *Flannery O'Connor: Collected Works*. New York: Library of America, 1988.

O'Neal, Hank. *"Life Is Painful, Nasty and Short…in My Case It Has Only Been Painful and Nasty."* New York: Paragon, 1990.

Patterson, David. *Literature and Spirit: Essays on Bakhtin and His Contemporaries*. Lexington: University Press of Kentucky, 1988.

Pereira, Kim. *August Wilson and the African American Odyssey*. Urbana: University of Illinois Press, 1995.

Perry, Richard. *Montgomery's Children*. San Diego: Harcourt Brace, 1984.

Peterson, Nancy J. "Introduction: Canonizing Toni Morrison." *Modern Fiction Studies* 39 (1993): 461–79.

Philip, Marlene Nourbese. *She Tries Her Tongue: Her Silence Softly Breaks*. Charlottetown (Canada): Ragweed, 1989.

Pinckney, Darryl. *High Cotton*. New York: Farrar Straus Giroux, 1992.

Ponzio, Augusto. "Philosophy of Language and Semiotics in Michail Bachtin." *Russian Literature* 32 (1992): 393–416.

Price, Reynolds. [Review of *Song of Solomon*]. *The New York Times Book Review* 11 Sept. 1977: 1.

Proust, Marcel. *Remembrance of Things Past*. New York: Random House, 1924.

Publishers Weekly. 198.3 (July 20, 1970): 2–3.

Publishers Weekly. 213.5 (Jan. 30, 1978): 34, 42.

Rampersad, Arnold. "Slavery and the Literary Imagination: Du Bois's *The Souls of Black Folks*." In McDowell and Rampersad, *Slavery and the Literary Imagination* 104–24.

Richburg, Keith. *Out of America: A Black Man Confronts Africa*. New York: Basic, 1997.

Ricoeur, Paul. "The Metaphorical Process as Cognition, Imagination, and Feeling." *Critical Inquiry* 5 (1978): 146–58.

Roberts, Mathew. "Poetics Hermeutics Dialogics: Bakhtin and Paul de Man." In Morson and Emerson, *Rethinking Bakhtin: Extensions and Challenges* 115–34.

Samuels, Wilfred D., and Clenora Hudson-Weems. *Toni Morrison*. Boston: Twayne, 1990.

Schroeder, Aribert. "An Afro-American Woman Writer and Her Reviewers/Critics: Some Ideological Aspects in Current Criticism of Toni Morrison's Fiction." *Arbeiten aus Anglistik und Amerikanistik* 15.2 (1990): 109–25.

Scott, James B. *Djuna Barnes*. Boston: Twayne, 1976.

Shannon, Sandra. *The Dramatic Vision of August Wilson*. Washington: Howard University Press, 1995.

Shklovsky, Victor. "Art as Technique." *Russian Formalist Criticism: Four Essays*. Tr. Lee T. Lemon and Marion J. Rice. 1917. Lincoln: University of Nebraska Press, 1965.

Singer, Alan. "The Horse Who Knew Too Much: Metaphor and the Narrative of Discontinuity in *Nightwood*." *Contemporary Literature* 25.1 (1984): 66–87.

————. "The Voice of History / The Subject of the Novel." *Novel* 21 (1988): 173–79.

Smith, Valerie. *Self-Discovery and Authority in Afro-American Narrative.* Cambridge: Harvard University Press, 1987.

Steele, Meili. *Critical Confrontations: Literary Theories in Dialogue.* Columbia: University of South Carolina Press, 1997.

————. "Metatheory and the Subject of Democracy in the Work of Ralph Ellison." *New Literary History* 27.3 (1996): 473-502.

Stepto, Robert. *From Behind the Veil: A Study of Afro-American Narrative.* Urbana: University of Illinois Press, 1991.

Strouse, Jean. "Toni Morrison's Black Magic." *Newsweek* 97 (30 March 1981): 52–56.

Taylor, Clyde. "Black Writing as Immanent Humanism." *The Southern Review* 21.3 (1985): 790–800.

Toomer, Jean. *Cane.* 1923. New York: Harper and Row, 1951.

Van Vechten, Carl. *Nigger Heaven.* New York: Knopf, 1926.

Voloshinov, V. N. *Marxism and the Philosophy of Language.* Tr. Ladislav Matejka and I. R. Titunik. 1930. New York: Seminar, 1973.

Walker, Alice. "Everyday Use." *In Love and Trouble: Stories of Black Women.* New York: Harcourt Brace, 1973.

Werner, Craig. "August Wilson's Burden: The Function of Neoclassical Jazz." In Nadel, *May All Your Fences Have Gates: Essays on the Drama of August Wilson* 21–50.

West, Cornell. *Keeping Faith: Philosophy and Race in America.* New York: Routledge, 1993.

Wheatley, Phillis. *Poems on Various Subjects, Religious and Moral.* London: Bell, 1773.

White, Edmund. "Black Like Whom?" *New York Times Book Review* 2 Feb. 1992: 3.

Wilson, August. *Fences.* New York: New American Library, 1986.

————. *Jitney!* Opened at Pittsburgh's Public Theater, 1982.

————. *Joe Turner's Come and Gone.* New York: Penguin, 1988.

————. *King Hedley II.* Opened at New York's Virginia Theater, 2001.

————. *Ma Rainey's Black Bottom.* New York: New American Library, 1985.

————. *The Piano Lesson.* New York: Dutton, 1990.

————. *Seven Guitars*. New York: Dutton, 1996.

————. *Two Trains Running*. New York: Plume, 1992.

Wisker, Gina. "'Disremembered and Unaccounted For': Reading Toni Morrison's *Beloved* and Alice Walker's *The Temple of My Familiar*." In Wisker, *Black Women's Writing* 78–90.

————. "Introduction. Black and White: Voices, Writers and Readers." In Wisker, *Black Women's Writing* 1–14.

Wisker, Gina, ed. *Black Women's Writing*. New York: St. Martin's, 1993.

Wittgenstein, Ludwig. *Zettel*. Oxford: Blackwell, 1976.

Wood, Ralph. *The Comedy of Redemption: Christian Faith and Comic Vision in Four American Novelists*. Notre Dame: University of Notre Dame Press, 1988.

Wright, Richard. "Blueprint for Negro Writing." *New Challenge* 2 (fall 1937): 53–65.

Zebroski, James Thomas. *Thinking through Theory: Vygotskian Perspectives on the Teaching of Writing*. Portsmouth, NH: Boynton/Cook, 1994.

Index